Martyn Payne joined the Barnabas children's ministry team in January 2003, having worked with CMS (Church Mission Society) for eight years as their National Children's Work Coordinator. Prior to his time with CMS, Martyn worked for 18 years as a teacher in East London. His published books for Barnabas include *A-cross the World*, *Footsteps to the Feast*, *Bethlehem Carols Unpacked* and *The People's Bible*.

Barnabas for Children ® is a registered word mark and the logo is a registered device mark of The Bible Reading Fellowship.

Published by
The Bible Reading Fellowship
15 The Chambers, Vineyard
Abingdon OX14 3FE
United Kingdom
Tel: +44 (0)1865 319700
Email: enquiries@brf.org.uk
Website: www.brf.org.uk
BRF is a Registered Charity

ISBN 978 1 84101 812 6
First published 2011
10 9 8 7 6 5 4 3 2 1 0
All rights reserved

Acknowledgments
Unless otherwise stated, scripture quotations are taken from the Contemporary English Version of the Bible published by HarperCollins Publishers, copyright © 1991, 1992, 1995 American Bible Society.

Scripture quotations taken from The Revised Standard Version of the Bible, copyright © 1946, 1952, 1971 by the Division of Christian Education of the National Council of the Churches of Christ in the United States of America, are used by permission. All rights reserved.

The paper used in the production of this publication was supplied by mills that source their raw materials from sustainably managed forests. Soy-based inks were used in its printing and the laminate film is biodegradable.

A catalogue record for this book is available from the British Library

Printed in Singapore by Craft Print International Ltd

The Big Story

36 session outlines and reflective Bible stories
exploring six big themes of God's love

Martyn Payne

Acknowledgments

Thanks to all those children and adults who experienced some of The Big Story reflective stories and outlines in their first incarnation and whose responses and comments have helped to shape this book.

Thanks, also, to the Barnabas children's ministry team, past and present, for their creative input to the stories:

Esther Chilvers

Jane Butcher

Alison Harris

Lucy Moore

'Everything in the Scriptures is God's Word. All of it is useful for teaching and helping people and for correcting them and showing them how to live. The Scriptures train God's servants to do all kinds of good deeds.'
(2 Timothy 3:16–17)

Photocopy permission

Contents

Foreword

Anyone who has ever watched the faces of children light up as they engage with the spoken word knows the importance of storytelling. Long after facts become confused or information forgotten, the emotional investment in a well-told story remains.

Some of my favourite memories are of reading aloud to children. Knowing that words they couldn't yet read or names they found hard to pronounce were transformed into sentences with meaning was only the beginning. Characters take on form and begin to live; landscapes grow up around the characters and change from grey to every shade of every colour; vivid moving pictures are painted in the child's imagination. What once may have been just symbols on pieces of paper have become stories with meaning.

Reading the Bible to children presents some special opportunities as well as challenges. The Bible is set in a different time and place with traditions that belong to its own people. The events recorded are not always told in the sequence in which they happened. The one story that the Bible tells can too easily be lost in the detail of each apparently unconnected story that a child hears. Even if a child can absorb the whole 'big story' that the Bible tells, the questions of why it matters, what difference it makes and how it applies to readers today still remain.

In this book, Martyn Payne has adopted the approach used in *The Barnabas Children's Bible*, connecting the many events and characters in the unfolding story of God's love for the people he created, loved and redeemed. He has chosen great themes presented in the Bible to bring together stories from the Old and New Testaments, and then used reflective storytelling to help children access them more readily. Stories are brought to life using simple props, sound effects and atmospheric lighting, and children are encouraged to immerse themselves in the narrative and become involved in the action, to wonder about what they see and hear and to feel comfortable about asking questions and offering their own thoughts.

Ultimately the creative and thought-provoking approach adopted by Martyn Payne in *The Big Story* allows children to cultivate their listening skills, engage with Bible stories and explore their meaning. In so doing, their spiritual understanding will be developed and they will begin to apply what they learn to their own lives.

Rhona Davies
Author of The Barnabas Children's Bible

Introduction

Many of us who love the Bible are often saddened and frustrated that its stories are so little known and read, even by Christians. Even when it is read, there is sometimes a tendency just to focus on a few well-known stories, particularly when working with children. The result is that we are in danger of nurturing a faith that has a very patchy and disjointed understanding of our precious story. Both children and adults may be able to reel off a few stories that they know but may not have enough of an idea of how those stories fit together and where they come in the overall thread of the Bible. Many programmes and even sermon series reinforce this tendency with periodic focuses on particular themes, characters or books, leaving those participating with a lot of fragments of the Bible but no sense of the whole. Even the lectionary approach can lead to this confusion.

The Big Story uses an approach to the Bible that connects up the whole story and attempts to give an overview of God's purposes; an approach that sees the Bible not as a collection of unrelated, if inspiring, events but as an amazing and ordered revelation of God's love. *The Barnabas Children's Bible*, with its unique reordering of the stories into a proper timeline, has inspired the development of materials that can help children and their leaders gain this bigger perspective.

The Big Story puts together a series of stories and ideas based on some big Bible themes. Each big theme is introduced by a reflective story to set the scene, then steps back and connects up six related individual stories from across the Bible. The reflective story is key to this approach. It can be used in a variety of ways to suit individual groups and the time available. For example, it could be used as a stand-alone story to begin thinking about special times of year, such as Advent and Lent; it can be used to give an overview before picking out two or three of the individual stories to accompany it over a few weeks, or it can be used in conjunction with its six individual stories as the basis for a children's activity day or holiday club. Equally, the programme would fit into a three-term year, with one big theme being explored in each half-term period.

The big themes explore:

Theme 1: Enemies and friends
Season: Start of the new school year
Introduction: Reflective story
1. Jacob and Esau (*Barnabas Children's Bible* stories 22–28)
2. Joseph and his brothers (*Barnabas Children's Bible* stories 28, 30, 31 and 37–39)
3. David and Jonathan (*Barnabas Children's Bible* stories 122–136)
4. The good Samaritan (*Barnabas Children's Bible* story 279)
5. Seventy times seven (*Barnabas Children's Bible* story 286)
6. Judas' betrayal (*Barnabas Children's Bible* story 305)

Theme 2: Dark and light
Season: Advent
Introduction: Reflective story
1. The story of Moses (*Barnabas Children's Bible* stories 45–66)
2. Deborah and Barak (*Barnabas Children's Bible* story 88)
3. The story of Elijah (*Barnabas Children's Bible* stories 162–169)
4. Isaiah's vision (*Barnabas Children's Bible* story 194)
5. The story of Jesus (*Barnabas Children's Bible* stories 247–252 and 278)
6. Paul's conversion (*Barnabas Children's Bible* story 326)

Theme 3: Famine and feast
Season: New year
Introduction: Reflective story
1. Manna and quails (*Barnabas Children's Bible* story 52)
2. Poverty and riches (*Barnabas Children's Bible* story 64)
3. The widow's oil (*Barnabas Children's Bible* story 163)
4. The wedding at Cana (*Barnabas Children's Bible* story 258)
5. Feeding the 5000 (*Barnabas Children's Bible* story 275)
6. The last supper (*Barnabas Children's Bible* story 303)

Theme 4: Death and life

Season: Lent to Easter

Introduction: Reflective story

1. Noah's ark (*Barnabas Children's Bible* stories 6, 7 and 8)
2. The bronze serpent (*Barnabas Children's Bible* story 68)
3. The dry bones (*Barnabas Children's Bible* stories 222–225)
4. The widow's son (*Barnabas Children's Bible* story 267)
5. Lazarus is brought back to life (*Barnabas Children's Bible* story 285)
6. The story of Easter (*Barnabas Children's Bible* story 308–311)

Theme 5: Depths and heights

Season: Easter to Pentecost

Introduction: Reflective story

1. Jeremiah in the well (*Barnabas Children's Bible* story 211)
2. Esther's prayer (*Barnabas Children's Bible* stories 227–231)
3. Jonah runs away (*Barnabas Children's Bible* stories 186–190)
4. God's blessings (*Barnabas Children's Bible* story 262)
5. The transfiguration (*Barnabas Children's Bible* story 278)
6. The coming of the Holy Spirit (*Barnabas Children's Bible* stories 317 and 319)

Theme 6: Hide and seek

Season: Summer term

Introduction: Reflective story

1. God's promise (*Barnabas Children's Bible* story 13)
2. Jacob wrestles with God (*Barnabas Children's Bible* story 27)
3. God's gift to Solomon (*Barnabas Children's Bible* story 147)
4. Jesus is baptised (*Barnabas Children's Bible* story 255)
5. The storm on the lake (*Barnabas Children's Bible* story 270)
6. John's vision (*Barnabas Children's Bible* story 363)

After a general introduction to the theme, and a reflective story, the expanded structure for each story in the theme is as follows:

- Bible links
- 'You will need' list
- The Barnabas Children's Bible story units
- Background to the story
- Open the story
- Tell the story
- Talk about the story
- Play with the story
- Reflect on the story

'The story of the story' on pages 10–12 is a stand-alone piece that explores how God's special book came together in the first place. This reflective story acts thus as a timeline that can help put all of the subsequent stories into a context and give a sense of the history behind the Bible's pages.

In conclusion, the Bible's big picture of God's love is such an amazing resource to nurture our faith that we need to invest time in finding creative ways to pass a love of the Bible on to our children. Many of us remember those who first gave us a feel for the Bible and are grateful for those who helped us to find our own story written there. The 'big theme' approach represented by *The Big Story* is offered in the same spirit of commitment to God's word.

The story of the story

The following reflective story stands on its own and is designed to give children a bird's eye view of how the Bible came together, as well as a three-dimensional timeline of Bible history. Ideally, it could be used at the beginning of a new academic year and then perhaps be revisited at the end of the following summer term. The intention is to provide a visual framework and point of reference for all the subsequent sessions and to capture the big picture of how God's story fits together. You may wish to display an enlarged picture of the story cloth so that subsequent story themes can be located in relation to the whole Bible. An enlargement of the image displayed on the inside cover of this book can be downloaded from the website: www.barnabasinchurches.org.uk/pdfs/thebigstory.pdf.

Members of the Barnabas children's ministry team often use the story in church training events and Barnabas RE Days in schools. Children's leaders, teachers and the children themselves have found it fascinating and it provokes some creative discussions. It is also used as a tool for the 400th birthday celebrations of the publication of the King James Version of the Bible (the Authorised Version) both at INSET events with primary teachers and in RE Days with children on the theme of 'What's so special about the Bible?' Visit www.barnabasinschools.org.uk for more details.

'The story of the story' is intended to give a visual framework and point of reference for all the sessions in the book, helping children to catch the big picture of how the Big Story all fits together.

You will need:

- A sand-coloured base cloth that rolls out 1m long by 23cm wide and is marked off into eight equal sections with seven thin pieces of wood (blunted kebab sticks, for example), so that when it is rolled up, the whole has the appearance of an ancient scroll.
- A small pottery dish filled with bits of broken wood and some tiny red and yellow beads to give the appearance of a glowing camp fire.
- A red heart-shaped tray holding ten flat, grey stones, each with a key word from one of the Ten Commandments scratched on it.
- A small gold box, large enough to contain the stones.

- Two tablets made from air-drying clay, marked to look as if there is writing on them.
- Some pieces of hand-made paper to represent papyrus.
- A Torah scroll made from two small rolling pin-like pieces of wood with hand-made paper rolled around them, on which are written one or two Hebrew words (search via the internet); paint the ends of the scroll gold and place in a small gold box.
- Eight small scrolls in a flat gold box (the staircase rods from a doll's house accessories pack make useful ends for these).
- One larger scroll, to represent the book of Isaiah.
- One or two pages of the early manuscripts of John's Gospel (Greek New Testament) photocopied on to stiff brown card and stapled together to represent the first codices on vellum (animal hide), and placed in a small silver envelope.
- More rolled-up scrolls of paper to represent the pastoral epistles.
- A mounted photocopy from one of the illustrated Latin manuscripts of the Bible (for example, a page from the Book of Kells), placed in a large silver envelope.
- A complete printed Bible.

Bible books: The stories of Genesis

Action: *Roll out one section of the base cloth from your right to your left.*

Script: In the beginning was the story.

Action: *Place the camp fire in the centre of the first section and trace a circle around it slowly, as you say the next words.*

Script: The people of God gathered in circles around their campfires in the desert. They did not need pictures or pages. In the glow of the fire they heard how the gift of light was given and how the darkness came, too. Beside their tents they listened to the story of the flood and were glad when the rainbow appeared. Beneath the stars they were told of Abram's long journey and the promise of the great family.

Bible books: The stories of Exodus, Leviticus, Numbers and Deuteronomy

Action: *Roll out the base cloth to reveal the second section. Bring out the red heart-shaped tray as you say the following.*

Script: After Moses had taken the people of God through the water into freedom, God gave him words to write down. The ten words were carved on stone tablets.

Action: *Put each of the ten flat stones down on the second section, saying the commandments as you do so. Put down the special gold box.*

Script: They kept this part of their story safe in a special box, which went everywhere with them.

Action: *Roll out the base cloth to reveal the third section.*

Script: When God's people came into the land they had been promised, they settled in towns and cities.

Action: *Place the two clay tablets on the third section, followed by the pieces of hand-made paper.*

Script: Here they began to write their stories down, first on clay tablets and then on a kind of paper made from reeds, called papyrus.

Action: *Roll out the base cloth to reveal the fourth section. Open the gold box and take out the Torah scroll.*

Script: The most important words from God were written on a great scroll. This part of the story is called the Torah. The priest read from it to the people whenever they worshipped God.

Action: *Open the Torah scroll to reveal the Hebrew writing.*

Bible books: The stories of Joshua, Judges, Ruth; the histories of Samuel, Kings and Chronicles; stories from Job, Proverbs, the Psalms and Song of Songs

Script: But they wanted to remember other stories, too, so they recorded these in the chronicles of the kings of Israel and Judah. They also wrote out the songs they sang, and some of the poems, that had become part of their story.

Action: *Place four of the smaller scrolls around the Torah.*

Bible books: The books of the prophets

Action: *Unroll the base cloth to reveal the fifth section.*

Script: Prophets are people who listen carefully for God's voice, and God speaks to them. They seem to know what God is thinking. The words of some of these prophets were put down on scrolls.

Action: *Place down the rest of the scrolls from the flat gold box, including the large one, which is the prophecy of Isaiah.*

Script: Now God's people could always read the warnings and the promises that God had given them.

Bible books: Luke 4:18–19; Isaiah 61:1–2

Action: *Point to several scrolls deliberately.*

Script: In the scrolls of the prophets, it was written that one day someone would come, who would be a king for ever. But he would be a king that no one expected.

Action: *Unroll the base cloth to reveal the sixth section.*

Script: When Jesus began his work in the synagogue at Nazareth, he read from the book of the prophet Isaiah, where it says…

Action: *Pick up the big scroll and unroll it, to read the following above the sixth section of the cloth, but afterwards replace the scroll on the fifth section, where it comes from.*

Script: The Lord's Spirit has come to me, because he has chosen me to tell good news to the poor. The Lord has sent me to announce freedom for prisoners, to give sight to the blind, to free everyone who suffers, and to say, 'This is the year the Lord has chosen.'

Bible books: Matthew, Mark, Luke and John

Script: Jesus did and said amazing things, and people did not want to forget his words. In the years after he had died and then had been seen alive again, some of his friends and followers wrote everything down on parchments.

Action: *Open the small silver envelope and show the parchment codex of John's Gospel, before placing it on the sixth section.*

Script: Now we too can read the Gospels and discover the story for ourselves.

Bible books: Acts and the pastoral letters from Paul, Peter, James, Jude and John to churches and individuals

Action: *Unroll the seventh section of the base cloth. Place down the rolled-up letter scrolls.*

Script: The story was taken across the sea and over the land. Christians wrote letters to each other and to the new churches.

Script: In each new country, God's people took great care to write the whole story down. The monks in Britain and Ireland made careful copies by hand, decorating each page with colourful pictures and beautiful writing. You can still see their manuscripts today.

Action: *Open the large silver envelope, and place down the copy of a page of an illuminated manuscript. Unroll the final section of the base cloth and place down the Bible.*

Script: Finally, the story was printed as a book. After many struggles and much hard work, it was produced in different languages. Some Bibles even have pictures and special notes to help people understand what is there. The story went out to the whole world and it is still travelling today. Look…

Action: *Pick up the Bible and hold it so that everyone can see it clearly.*

Script: It is all here in the Bible. It is a whole library of story books. Let's open the cover and let the stories out!

Action: *Open the Bible to reveal its many pages of stories. Holding it first over the camp fire section and then over each of the other sections of the base cloth in turn, flick through the pages of the Bible and say…*

Script: Here are the stories from the desert and the ten words from God…
          Here are the most important laws and the history of their kings…
          Here are the songs the people sang and the poems they wrote…
          Here are the warnings and the promises of the prophets…
          Here are the Gospels that tell the story of Jesus…
          Here are all the letters that the first Christian leaders wrote to help the church to go on sharing the story.
          In the beginning was the story.
          In the end there is still the story.
          Now we can all read the story for ourselves.
          And there is more. We, too, can become part of this story, part of God's big story. I wonder what our story will be?

 Reproduced with permission from *The Big Story* published by BRF 2011 (978 1 84101 812 6) **www.barnabasinchurches.org.uk**

— Theme 1 —

Enemies and friends

Season: Start of the new school year

General introduction to the theme

When God made people, one way in which we were like God was through our ability to offer and receive the gift of friendship. However, when we choose to betray that friendship with God, this gift becomes broken. People often choose to hate others, turning friends into enemies. But God never stops longing for friendship with and between all people. Jesus came into the world so that everyone could see the never-ending friendship that God offers. It is a friendship that is greater than the power of revenge, hatred and death. When Jesus rose from the dead, it was made available to anyone. Again and again, God shows through the stories in the Bible how hatred can be turned into love and enemies can become friends. This is the good news that Christians can pass on to a broken world.

Reflective overview

A Bible, 16 wooden people figures and one other distinct wooden figure to represent Jesus, a large circle of blue felt, small silver confetti hearts, a small model sheep, a small multi-coloured piece of cloth, a small crown, a small model donkey, a simple cross glued on to a heart-shaped base

Bible story: Genesis 1:1—2:4

Action: *Open the Bible and then lay it down at your side.*

Script: God has given us the stories in his book to show us what he is like and help us to discover how we are meant to live.

Action: *Lay down a large circle of light blue felt and scatter some small silver hearts over it.*

Script: When God made the world, he loved it and filled it with love.

Bible story: Genesis 3:1—4:16

Action: *Place twelve wooden figures in a circle around the centre of the felt.*

Script: God made people to be like him. He wanted them to care for the world and to love and care for each other.

Action: *Rearrange the twelve figures in three groups of four, but still close to the centre of the felt.*

Script: God gave people many gifts to do this caring, and one of the greatest of these was the gift of choosing to be friends: friends with God and friends with other people.

Action: *Reposition the figures as individuals around the whole world, randomly. As you place them down, turn them as if they are turning their backs on each other.*

Script: But people chose not to be friends with God and the gift was broken. Friends became enemies and God's world began to fill up with hatred alongside the love.

Bible story: Genesis 25:19—33:20

Action: *Move your right hand across the world as if searching for those who will be friends.*

Script: People chose to be enemies, not friends. But God never stopped wanting to be friends with the people he had made, and so he looked for those who would choose friendship, not hatred. God loved to call these people his friends.

Action: *In the near quarter of the world on the storyteller's left, reposition two of the figures opposite each other and put a model sheep in between them.*

Script: God saw how Jacob and his brother Esau became enemies over what belonged to them; but then God patiently worked in their lives to mend and to use what had been broken.

Bible story: Genesis 37 and 39—47

Action: *In the middle, on the storyteller's left, reposition two of the figures opposite each other and put the small piece of colourful cloth in between them.*

Script: God saw how Joseph and his brothers became enemies over Joseph's position in the family. Then God patiently worked in their lives to mend and to use what had been broken.

Bible story: 1 Samuel 18:1—20:42

Action: *Lower down on the storyteller's left, reposition three of the figures in a triangle and put a model crown in between them.*

Script: Although young David and King Saul's son Jonathan were friends, God saw how Saul and David became enemies. Then God worked in their lives to mend and to use what had been broken.

Bible story: John 3:16–17

Script: God longed that people would choose friendship with God and each other; but again and again they chose to become enemies instead.

Action: *Place a new, distinct but similar figure on the felt at the bottom, furthest from the storyteller.*

Script: Finally, Jesus came into the world to show us how to become God's friends again. Jesus was God's only Son. He showed God's love to everyone, even those who were treated as enemies and outsiders. Jesus is known as a friend to all.

Bible story: Luke 10:25–37

Action: *Low down on the felt, to the storyteller's right, reposition two new figures opposite each other, one lying flat, and put a model donkey in between them.*

Script: Once, Jesus told a story of how a hated enemy chose to become a surprising friend.

Bible story: Matthew 5:44–45

Action: *In the middle of the felt, on the storyteller's right, reposition three figures in a triangle, touching each one in turn as you speak the following words.*

Script: Jesus teaches people how to be friends with those who are different. He says that people should love their enemies into becoming friends. Jesus shows people how friends should forgive enemies. He says, 'Love your enemies and pray for anyone who ill-treats you. Then you will be acting like your Father in heaven.'

Bible story: Matthew 18:21–35

Script: How many times should you forgive someone who does you wrong? 'Not just seven times,' says Jesus, 'but seventy-seven times!'

Bible story: Matthew 26:47–50, 56

Script: But then God saw how people chose to hate Jesus and become his enemies. Even his closest friends turned away from him.

Bible story: John 15:13–15

Action: *Place a small cross with a heart-shaped base on the closest part of the felt to the storyteller's right. Gently, lay the cross down on its side.*

Script: God watched Jesus lay down his life for his friends and his enemies, to mend and to use what had been broken. 'The greatest way to show love for friends is to die for them... I speak to you as my friends,' says Jesus.

Bible story: 2 Corinthians 5:19–21

Action: *Pause, and then stand the cross upright.*

Script: But in Jesus, the gift of God's friendship proved stronger than hatred, more powerful than death.

Action: *Carefully place four new figures around the cross.*

Script: Now, because of Jesus' love, people can show the world how hatred can become love, how enemies can become friends, and how anyone can be called a friend of God.

Bible story: Proverbs 17:17; 18:24; 27:6

Action: *Sweep your right hand across the whole world.*

Script: Because God's friendship is for all those who put their trust in him.

Script: I wonder what is so special about friendship... and why people choose to become enemies, not friends.
I wonder what is so special about friendship with God... and how friendships can be mended.
I wonder how friendship can be stronger than hatred... and how hatred can be turned to love.

Double trouble

The story of Jacob and Esau

Bible links

Genesis 25:19–34; 27:1–45; 32:1—33:20

You will need:

A blindfold, fake fur fabric, raffia

— The Barnabas Children's Bible —

Stories 22–28

Background to the story

Jacob and Esau may have been twins but they had very different personalities and temperaments. They were opposites in so many ways—their appearance, their gifts and their tastes. What is more, their mum and dad disagreed over which son they liked the best. This was a recipe for a family disaster! Jacob and Esau should have been friends but instead they became deadly enemies.

Jacob took advantage of his brother, lying and cheating in order to ensure that he was the one who, with his father's blessing, would be in charge of the family business and fortune one day. Consequently, Jacob had to run for his life, in fear of Esau. Can God change such enemies into friends? Can God bring good out of such wickedness? Can God mend and use what is so broken? Through strange experiences in prayer and the long years of waiting and service away from home, Jacob's life was changed by God. The outcome of the story is that the Bible encourages us again and again to trust in the God of Jacob.

The following outline picks up on the theme of God reconciling the two brothers who became enemies. By the power of the Holy Spirit, God can turn hatred into love.

Open the story

Using some of the activities below, introduce the story of Jacob and Esau, particularly the incidents where Jacob tricks and takes advantage of his brother.

- Play a game in which one child is blindfolded and has to try to guess who comes to sit in the chair beside him or her, just by feeling hands and arms (carefully and respectfully). Add an extra dimension by wrapping the arms and hands of the child being identified in some furry material.
- Talk about the children's favourite foods. Just how much do they like these foods and to what lengths are they prepared to go to get them?
- Talk about what the children find fair and unfair in everyday life. What sorts of things cause tensions in the family… between brothers and sisters… between parents and children… and between friends? (NB: Be sensitive to the children and to what is shared.)

Link the activities to the sorry tale of what happened between Jacob and Esau.

Tell the story

Use the following sound effects and actions as scaffolding to link the events in Jacob's life as you tell the story.

- Baby crying sounds (the twins' birth)
- Slurping food noises (bargaining for the birthright)
- Stroking hands and hair (cheating to get the blessing)
- Running fast on the spot (running away from home)
- Sleeping noises (sleeping outdoors and then waking to see angels)
- A loud exclamation of 'Wow!' (marrying Laban's daughter)
- A distressed shout of 'Oh no!' (discovering that she is the wrong bride)
- Sheep noises (working on Laban's farm)
- A cry for help (fear at meeting Esau again)
- Wrestling and struggling sounds (wrestling with an angel)

Talk about the story

Make the point that the Bible contains some amazing stories. Can the children think of any? For example, there's Daniel the lion tamer, David the giant killer, Samson the strong man and Jacob the angel wrestler! Talk about the story by asking the following questions.

- Why did God send an angel to wrestle with Jacob?
- What did Jacob think the fight was all about?
- Why wouldn't Jacob let go?
- What was Jacob trying to prove?
- What did Jacob learn from this incident and from all the years he'd been away from home?

Explain that on his way back home, before Jacob met Esau, he also planned and prayed a lot. He sent gifts ahead, along with messengers. He was expecting the worst, but God had clearly been working in Esau's life too. Whenever enemies become friends again, we can guarantee that God is at work, mending and using what has been broken. In the story, Jacob says that seeing Esau's face is like seeing the face of God (Genesis 33:10).

I wonder what the whole story is trying to teach us today. What is God saying about friendship?

Play with the story

In groups, create the following items to go with the different events of the story.

- The recipe for Esau's favourite food and some illustrations to go with it.
- Isaac's last will and testament, with alterations giving everything to Jacob rather than Esau.
- A hand-and-arm wrap made out of raffia or some fake fur fabric, to deceive Isaac.
- Jacob's diary entries for the night he dreamt of angels… the day he got married to the wrong sister… the evening before he met Esau…
- A picture of the lentil stew pot.

Reflect on the story

Pray for situations, both local and global, where friends have become enemies; where people who live in the same country are at war with each other; where people who believe in the same God have nevertheless fallen out with each other; and where people have been forced to run away from home. Make the prayer visual by providing some small plastic or wooden figures and, whenever a particular prayer is made, placing two figures next to each other to symbolise enemies becoming friends.

Big brothers
The story of Joseph and his brothers

Bible links

Genesis 37; 39—47

You will need:

A CD of *Joseph and His Amazing Technicolor Dreamcoat*, masking tape, a large dice, snakes and ladders instruction cards (see below), thought-bubble cards, a piece of multicoloured fabric, craft and collage materials, a roll of plain wallpaper, small broken toys or household items to repair

— The Barnabas Children's Bible —

Stories 28, 30, 31 and 37–39

Background to the story

Joseph's father Jacob should have known better. He had experienced the negative result of favouritism in his own family home but, nevertheless, he repeated the same mistake. Of course he had loved Joseph's mum very much, but, by publicly valuing her sons over the other ten children, he was asking for a family disaster. Joseph was spoilt and became arrogant and proud. Understandably, his brothers became his enemies: the dreamer had to go. Yet, as Stephen comments in the book of Acts, 'God was with Joseph' (Acts 7:9).

God is at work in the lives of his people to bring about reconciliation, turning enemies into friends. After the long years in Egypt as a slave, a prisoner and then as prime minister, Joseph had a chance to test his brothers to see if they had changed and then, finally, a chance to become reunited with them. He saw God's hand at work in all this. As he said, 'You meant evil against me; but God meant it for good' (Genesis 50:20, RSV).

The following outline explores the story of a family feud that God used, in the end, to save his people from famine and to bring togetherness out of what had been torn apart.

Open the story

The Joseph story is well known, if only because of its recently revised appearance in London's West End. Obtain a CD of the musical and play one or two tracks to help the children into the story. They may even know some of the lyrics.

We know that Joseph was the favourite son in his large family. The Bible story tells us of the special coat he was given, but I wonder what other privileges Joseph enjoyed? From the children's own experiences of family rivalries and jealousies, ask them to suggest some of the other things that may have contributed to the build-up of resentment towards Joseph from his elder brothers.

Tell the story

Joseph's life is a dramatic series of ups and downs. The following activity uses the idea of a game similar to snakes and ladders, which charts the fall and rise of Joseph.

Set out a grid on the floor that is six squares by six squares. Each square should be large enough to take an instruction card as well as space for one, two or even three children to stand. Use ready-made noughts and crosses grids—for example, those that are available from the Early Learning Centre. The sets consist of nine foam squares that interlock (3 x 3) to show a noughts and crosses grid on one side and a snakes and ladders game on the other. If you join together four of these sets, you will have a grid of 36 squares (6 x 6). Alternatively, just use masking tape and create your own grid on the floor.

You will also need a large dice (there is a blow-up dice in the ELC pack, or one is available separately).

You need to attach a set of instruction cards (see page 19) to your game area or fix them within the squares of the grid. Starting with the bottom left-hand square, the path through the grid travels left to right, then right to left, and so on, zigzagging its way to finish in the top left-hand square. Distribute the instruction cards evenly among the 36 squares, placing them in the order given below. Before you start the game, check the spacing of the cards to ensure that the children are not being forced to move forward or back on to yet another instruction card.

Depending on the size of the group, you should be able to have up to three or four children playing the game at one time. The others can watch and ensure fair play while they await their turn. The winners of the different heats could then play each other. By then, the facts and events in the life of Joseph should have been covered at least once.

Instruction cards

The first card should be placed in the bottom left-hand square of the grid:

1. The downs and ups of Joseph
Throw an even number to start

2. Jacob's favourite son
Move forward 2

3. Joseph dreams he's top dog
Move forward 2

4. Joseph is resented by his brothers
Move back 1

5. Jacob gives Joseph a special coat
Move forward 2

6. Joseph grasses on his brothers
Move back 1

7. Joseph's brothers resent him even more
Move back 1

8. Joseph's brothers throw him in a pit
Move back 3

9. The brothers sell Joseph to Ishmaelite traders
Move back 1

10. Joseph works for Potiphar in Egypt
Move forward 2

11. Potiphar's wife lies about Joseph. He is slung into jail
Move back 1

12. Joseph interprets dreams for the king's cook and personal servant
Move forward 1

13. The king's personal servant forgets about Joseph—two more years in jail
Miss a turn

14. Pharaoh has dreams and Joseph is sent for
Move forward 1

15. Joseph ends up as governor of Egypt
Move forward 2

16. Joseph's brothers come looking for grain. Can Joseph forgive them?
Miss a turn

17. Joseph tests his brothers. Have they changed? Yes!
Move forward 1

18. Joseph invites his family to stay in Egypt
Hurray!

The final card should go in the top left-hand square of the grid:

Talk about the story

The suggested activities below focus on different aspects of Joseph's story. Use one or more of these activities to talk about the issues involved in Joseph's big family drama.

- Act out Joseph's two dreams, set in the cornfields and in the night sky (Genesis 37:5–9). Freeze the scene at the point when everyone bows down to Joseph, and interview Joseph's brothers about what they are thinking at that moment.
- After his brothers had thrown Joseph into the pit, there must have been a heated debate among them over what to do next. We know that Reuben hoped to save him. The others must have had other ideas. Starve him to death? Hope he died from snakebite, sunstroke or a landslide? Should they stone him or sell him? Gather the children around an imaginary campfire in a circle to debate what to do next with Joseph. Pass around a piece of coloured cloth to represent Joseph's coat as each child is invited to speak.
- Once Joseph has become prime minister, it is his turn to make decisions about the fate of his big brothers. He reacts first with a mixture of revenge and remorse, often having to turn away to hide his tears. I wonder what thoughts were going through his mind at the time? Pass around the outline of

a large thought bubble for the children to make suggestions about what Joseph might have been thinking when he had his brothers in his power. When friends become enemies, inevitably there will be thoughts of getting our own back. The story recognises this.

Play with the story

Use craft or collage materials to create Joseph's coat, the two dreams, and Joseph's interpretation of the dreams. Work as a group on a length of plain wallpaper, or let the children work individually on sheets of paper.

Reflect on the story

As a way to anchor the story, collect some toys or small household items that are broken (but repairable) in some way. Distribute the items and, as each one is repaired (though perhaps not easily, and probably with help), use this as a way to pray for broken situations between people that the children might like to name or think about quietly.

In the palace, Joseph said to Pharaoh, 'I can't... but God can' (Genesis 41:16). Use this as a repeated five-word prayer (one word for each digit of the left hand) as the items are repaired.

In Egypt, Joseph named his second son Ephraim. This name means 'fruitful despite everything'. In other words, Joseph was saying, 'God brings good from bad'. Use this as a second five-word prayer (one word for each digit on the right hand) as a way of anchoring the story.

A friend indeed
The story of David and Jonathan

Bible links

1 Samuel 18:1–3; 20:1–42; 2 Samuel 1:17–27; 9:1–13

You will need:

Different-coloured strips of fabric to make friendship bands, a toy bow and arrow, numbered envelopes, the story from 1 Samuel 20 printed off and cut into ten sections

— The Barnabas Children's Bible —

Stories 122 and 136

Background to the story

David was a person who was dear to God's heart (Acts 13:22). He understood about the gift of friendship and tried both to make friends and to be a friend all his life. Of course, he also made many mistakes but he knew God wanted him to choose to be friends, not enemies, with other people. Even when King Saul turned against him after the defeat of Goliath, David did not choose hatred. We see David's capacity for friendship best in his relationship with Saul's son, Jonathan, with whom he made a lifelong pact (a covenant) of commitment. This was worked out both when Jonathan saved David's life and, much later, when David cared for Jonathan's crippled son, Mephibosheth, rather than taking revenge on Saul's descendants. David even refused to raise his hand against King Saul, who had chosen to hate David, sparing Saul's life when it would have been very easy to choose the way of violence instead (1 Samuel 24).

When David heard of Saul's and Jonathan's deaths in battle, it broke his heart.

From David's life, the following outline picks up the theme of friendship in the face of hatred, focusing on two incidents in particular.

Open the story

Discuss with the children how friends mark their friendship with each other. Is it through exchanging gifts… making promises… a special ceremony… making friendship bracelets, or something else? Talk about what it means to have friends. What makes a best friend and how do friends prove their friendship?

Explain how Jonathan and David became friends following Goliath's defeat. They stayed friends all their lives, despite enormous pressures and dangers. Have a discussion about colours that we might associate with lifelong friendship. What is the sign of God's friendship towards us? Is it a rainbow… a cross… or something else?

Tell the story

David ends up on the run from King Saul and relies on Saul's son, Jonathan, for inside information about approaching danger (1 Samuel 20), but at a cost: Jonathan almost gets himself killed. David and Jonathan arrange a secret signal between them that will let David know whether Saul means to kill him or not. The signal is that Jonathan will shoot three arrows and then communicate to David through the instructions he gives for the arrows to be retrieved by a servant (vv. 20–22).

Divide up the story in 1 Samuel 20 into ten sections. Put each section into numbered envelopes and pin the envelopes to a noticeboard, which should be placed at one end of the meeting area and away from anything breakable. Using a toy bow and arrow (with a rubber tip), ask everyone in turn to try to hit the envelopes in the correct sequence. As each envelope is hit, it is opened and that part of the story read out.

Talk about the story

The depth of David and Jonathan's friendship was proved much later by the way David acted towards Jonathan's son, Mephibosheth (2 Samuel 9). David didn't have to show such kindness, but he did. Read the story and then discuss how true friends are prepared to go out of their way for each other. What a surprise it must have been to David's court to see him acting in this way towards Mephibosheth. To what lengths will true friends go to help each other? Hand out some post-it 'speech bubbles' and ask the children to complete the phrase, 'Friendship means…'. Compare notes and discuss what has been written.

The depth of the friendship between David and Jonathan is shown particularly in David's reaction to Saul's death in battle. Read 2 Samuel 1:17–27. It would have been extraordinary at that time to show such sorrow over an enemy's death. Such sadness was the mark of being a true friend. Imagine what David's army officers would have said when they saw their king in tears.

Set up a debate between those who think David was right to mourn Saul's and Jonathan's deaths and those who think it was a sign of weakness.

Play with the story

Make friendship bands using different-coloured strips of fabric. Link the activity to the colour suggestions made in the 'Open the story' discussions.

Reflect on the story

Ask the children to write out the names of all their friends on separate pieces of paper and then arrange them randomly in a circle. Place a candle in the middle. Now ask everyone to choose a name other than one they have written and call it out, so that all the friends are named before God in a prayer of thanksgiving and blessing.

Shock horror
The story of the good Samaritan

Bible link

Luke 10:25–37

You will need:

Optical illusions, ribbon, cardboard circles and tin foil, outline figures made out of paper

— The Barnabas Children's Bible —

Story 279

Background to the story

The story of the good Samaritan is so familiar that we can easily allow it to lose its original impact. The hatred between Jews and Samaritans was intense—a Jew would not even allow a Samaritan's shadow to fall across his path—and Jesus knew that he was stirring up a real hornet's nest by casting a Samaritan in the role of the third passer-by.

The lawyer who asked Jesus the question, 'Who are my neighbours?' (Luke 10:29) wanted to probe into whom we should care for as our neighbour. As the first part of Jesus' story unfolded, it seemed to be leading to the acceptable truth that anyone in need is our neighbour—even if the circumstances are risky. But the twist is that it is only the outsider who understands this truth. Respectable Jews missed the point. What's more, the man in need had to be willing to receive help from someone whose shadow almost certainly fell across him. As we see often in the Gospels, outsiders are more attuned to God's kingdom than so-called insiders. They seem to know that true compassion turns enemies into friends and thus shows how this world was meant to be.

The following outline explores the upside-down thinking about enemies and friends that the parable introduces.

Open the story

Jesus' parables are stories designed to bring us up short and make us think again. They take an unexpected twist or illustrate a surprising paradox, in order to get us thinking afresh about God's kingdom. In some ways, they are a bit like optical illusions. We think we see what's there, but then suddenly we realise that there is something else too. Show some pictures of illusions, downloaded from the internet (for example, the website www.sightsavers.org).

Tell the story

Sit the children in a circle. Explain that the circle is the story circle and that when you start telling the story, the children must put up their hands if they would like to act it out. Choose some of the first volunteers to go into the circle and mime the story. When you wave your arms over the circle, this clears the circle and the first volunteers must sit back in their places. Others are then chosen to carry on acting out the story.

Keep clearing the circle so that the children know they can all have a chance to act, and that clearing doesn't mean they have failed in some way. Include lots of actions in your storytelling: for example, say, 'He grinned from ear to ear' rather than 'He was happy'.

Don't force anyone to act, as some children may prefer to watch. Retell the parable with lots of action and added details about the journey, the dangers on the road and the reactions of the passers-by. (NB: When the robbers attack, they are pretend-fighting an invisible traveller.)

Talk about the story

Choose three children to play the three passers-by and put the remaining children into two groups. One group suggests reasons why each passer-by should stop to help and the other group suggests reasons why they shouldn't. Be prepared for some interesting insights. Ask the passers-by which inner voice of conscience he or she will follow.

Talk about ideas for the children's own version of the story that they can tell together. A modern-day version would need to use two characters who should know what to do for someone in need, and one who is a deadly enemy of the person in trouble.

Stretch the children's thinking about the story by asking them what might have happened or might have been said later. For example:

- What did the innkeeper tell his friends about his overnight guests?
- What did the Samaritan say to his family to explain why he was so late arriving in Jericho?
- How did the poor mugged traveller come to terms with having to receive help from a dreaded enemy?
- What did one 'look-out thief', who was left behind, think about the different travellers' reactions?

Turning enemies into friends is often about who is prepared to make the first move and what prompts them to do so. In the Samaritan's case, the story says that he felt sorry for the injured man (Luke 10:33), which moved him to do something completely out of the ordinary. Why do the children think that, on this occasion, the Samaritan was prepared to act out of character towards the Jewish person? What should inspire Christians to care in this sort of way for others?

Play with the story

- In Britain, those who do good deeds for others in peace time are awarded a medal known as the George Cross. Design and produce a medal for the Samaritan in recognition of what he did for the injured man. You will need ribbon and cardboard circles covered with tin foil, on to which you can put your design and any appropriate wording, such as 'Treat others as you want them to treat you' (Matthew 7:12).
- Teach some simple first-aid skills, such as learning to put someone in the recovery position or making a simple sling, as an activity linked to the story.
- Explore the origins of the organisation known as the Samaritans (www.samaritans.org), which is an example of how Christians and others choose to act differently.

Reflect on the story

Think about those who are considered outsiders today. Pray that kind consideration and the work of God's Spirit may help people to act out of character and turn enemies into friends. To symbolise this during the prayers, move some simple outline figures from the edge of the circle into the middle. Invite the children to change their hands from a fist shape into a high-five greeting with those on either side of them.

Friendship is forgiving
The story of the official who refused to forgive

Bible link

Matthew 18:21–35

You will need:

A large dice, coins, craft materials, empty tissue boxes, tin foil, collage materials, paper strips to make paper chains

— The Barnabas Children's Bible —

Story 286

Background to the story

The encouragement to be at peace with everyone—to be friends, not enemies—is all very well, but what happens when people hurt others again and again? Some enemies just don't seem to want to become friends! This is at the heart of the very practical question that Peter puts to Jesus: aren't some people and some situations simply unforgivable?

Jesus tackles this important question by telling a story. It is a story about what forgiveness is like in God's scheme of things. The truth is that we are all like the servant who owed millions. There are so many reasons why we, too, are in no position to be friends of the king, but God's mercy makes forgiveness possible. The servant is forgiven, but this forgiveness should be passed on.

Peter and the others who heard the story for the first time would have reacted with anger at the way the pardoned servant treated those who were dependent on him. It's obvious that those who receive mercy should pass it on—and so Peter has his answer!

Because of God's love poured out to us through Jesus, we are forgiven and, as we are reminded in the Lord's Prayer, this means that we ought to forgive others. In this way, enemies can become friends.

Open the story

Introduce the topic of forgiveness and its relationship to turning enemies into friends, by making or adapting a dice. Print off some labels to stick on to the different sides with the following phrases.

- I find it hard to forgive others when…
- I find it hard to forgive others because…
- I find… unforgivable.
- I would forgive others but…
- I can only forgive others if…
- True forgiveness means…

Ask the children in turn to throw the dice and then to complete the sentence on the face that is uppermost. This should get some discussion going.

Tell the story

Make the point of the parable visible by piling up lots of coins of different denominations on one side of a table and another, but much smaller, pile of just a few pence on the other side. Point to the two piles as you retell the story.

Now ask the children to imagine how they might react to being let off from one or the other of the different amounts by a bank or credit company. How might they feel about it? Help them to unravel the meaning of the story for themselves by using some of the following questions for discussion.

- I wonder why the king let off the official with the big debt…
- I wonder how the forgiven official felt…
- I wonder how his family felt…
- I wonder why he then behaved so differently towards the other man…
- I wonder what the other officials in the story thought of him…
- I wonder what Jesus means by his comment that we should forgive with all our hearts… (Matthew 18:35)

Talk about the story

As a group, try to put together some estimated costs on a bill for some of the things that we enjoy each day but that have no market value, such as the air we breathe, our friendships and family, good health, beautiful scenery, wonderful parks and gardens to visit, new sights and sounds to enjoy, and so on. Draw up an imaginary price list for all these things and then, in bold letters across the whole list, write: 'No charge, with love from God'. What consequences might God's free gifts have for our relationship with him and the people around us?

Read together Matthew 6:9–15 (the Lord's Prayer). Why does Jesus add a further comment on the section about forgiving others?

Unwillingness to forgive creates barriers between people, which grow harder and harder to break down, the longer the situation is allowed to continue. Read what Jesus had to say about this in Matthew 5:25–26.

Back in the Genesis story, following the murder of Abel by Cain, the breakdown in that friendship led to tenfold revenge (Genesis 4:24). Jesus turns this whole idea upside down by speaking of a 70 times sevenfold forgiveness (Matthew 18:22). Discuss with the children whether they think that this is really practical and possible. Now look at Matthew 5:43–44, where we're told that we should forgive even our enemies. How can we ever hope to do this seemingly impossible thing?

Play with the story

- Cover and decorate an empty tissue box to create a treasure chest in which the king in the story might have kept his wealth. Fill it with circles of tin foil to represent the 50 million silver coins that he had lent his official.
- Hide 100 pennies around the meeting space and give the children a time limit within which to find all the coins. At the end of the allotted time, have a discussion about how the man in the story might have felt when he couldn't pay back his small debt to the official who refused to forgive.
- Create a group collage of a giant pair of scales. On one side, fill the highest weighing pan with a huge debt of coins. Show that this is easily outweighed by filling the pan on the other side with the word 'forgiveness' in chunky bold lettering.

Reflect on the story

Friendship is forgiving, but forgiving others doesn't come easily. It's like building a paper chain, link by link. Every time we forgive, we strengthen the possibility of an eventual total link-up. On some paper chains, write symbols or words for those things that build barriers between people, such as distrust, harsh words, fear, ignorance, unfairness, jealousy, hurt and anger. Link up all the chains and then create a forgiveness chain by drawing a very deliberate cross over each word as a reminder that Jesus has forgiven us for all these things. Reflect on how the cross is the source of our strength to link up in friendship and forgiveness with others. In a circle, hold the chain and pray together the key line from the Lord's Prayer: 'forgive us for doing wrong as we forgive others' (Matthew 6:12).

The kiss of death

The story of Jesus' betrayal by a friend

Bible link

Matthew 26:47–56

You will need:

A set of blank cards (one marked with an X), a set of friendship bracelets, a large picture of Jesus' betrayal, the letters of the word 'friendship' written on separate pieces of card

— The Barnabas Children's Bible —

Story 305

Background to the story

Jesus experienced the full force of broken friendship in the garden of Gethsemane when he was betrayed by Judas and arrested. He had offered friendship with God to all who came to him but now that friendship was thrown back in his face. The tide turned and people chose to become his enemies instead. Only hours before, in the upper room, he had told his disciples that they were his friends: so great was his love that he would lay down his life for them. But Jesus' friendship was betrayed by a kiss. He was then denied by one of his closest friends and abandoned by the rest. Jesus took the pain of broken friendship to the grave and then, through his resurrection, made available the power to choose a never-ending friendship with God. He tasted the destruction of friendship in order to mend what had been broken for the whole world.

Open the story

Play one or two of the following games to try to capture some of the experiences of that night in Gethsemane.

- Let the children take it in turns to ask for help from the rest of the group. As the person in need approaches the others (one at a time) to ask for help, each child should deliberately and unemotionally turn away and face the other direction. Continue until everyone has ignored the request and turned his or her back to the one asking for help. Make sure several of the children experience being the person in need.

- Prepare a set of cards, one card for each child. Only one card has an X on it. Deal out the cards randomly, then ask the children to look at their own card to find out, in secret, whether or not they are the one with the X—the betrayer. Now ask them to walk around the room, shaking hands or giving a high-five greeting to everyone else. After half a minute of greetings, everyone should sit down where they are and then try to guess who the betrayer is. It was someone they greeted. The betrayer must try to make sure nobody guesses that it was him or her. Ask the children what it feels like to know that someone with whom they have been enjoying a game is actually a traitor. Let several people have a go at being the secret betrayer so as not to stigmatise anybody in that role.

- Set the children off, milling about the room calmly, but then suddenly call out one person's name. Now all the rest should do their best to avoid that one person and isolate them, keeping as far away as possible. Freeze the situation and explore how it feels to be deserted like this. Make sure you do it again, calling out other children to be the isolated ones, so that no one feels got at.

Tell the story

Tell the story of Gethsemane from a hidden spectator's point of view. Set up some covered chairs around the meeting place to represent bushes and trees in the garden for the children to hide behind. Also, darken the room as much as you can. Tell the children that they are observers of the story, late at night on the Thursday before Easter. Jesus arrives just after midnight with his friends, hoping to find some time to pray.

Focus on the different sounds that the hidden spectators will probably hear from behind the bushes, including several footsteps coming through the undergrowth; a settling down in a group among the leaves and roots of the olive trees; a few people walking off alone (Jesus and his three closest disciples); the groans of a prayer; particular words from the prayer, namely 'not my will but yours be done'; the sound of snoring; later, the sound of marching feet approaching; the sound of a kiss; sounds of fighting; sounds of people running away and soldiers marching away. Occasionally stop the narrative to invite the children to say how they feel about what they are hearing.

Next, as a painful visual aid for this story, collect together some attractive friendship bracelets, preferably twelve of them. Then, if you can bear it, cut them up as you explore with the children how Jesus' friends let him down. Use the torn and jagged pieces of the friendship bracelets to make a cross shape as a link to what happens on Good Friday.

Talk about the story

Jesus experienced being thoroughly let down that night. Judas gave him a kiss, which should have been a sign of affection but, in fact, was the cue for Jesus' arrest. The disciples all ran away, and later, in the courtyard near where Jesus was being tried, Peter denied even knowing him. Ask the children to suggest qualities they associate with being a true friend and then to compare those qualities with the events and the reactions of the disciples that night. Jesus knew all about friendship that fails. Why might it be that this story is recorded for us as part of the Easter story?

Play with the story

Choose a well-known picture of Jesus' betrayal (via an internet image search). Show the picture or, if possible, project it on to a wall or screen. Bring the picture to life by asking the children to recreate a living tableau of the scene. Some could be the directors who decide on props and the positions of the actors. Add in movement and dialogue, and work out the order of events. This is an imaginative way to explore the story from the inside.

Reflect on the story

Gather in a circle and place the letter cards showing the word 'friendship' in the centre. Pray about friends who have fallen out with each other, breaking up the word and scattering the letters around randomly as you do so. Next, place the letters in a cross shape and ask Jesus to help those who experience broken friendships. Finally, reshape the letters to resemble a human figure and thank Jesus for his promise that he will help us to remake friendships as they should be.

— Theme 2 —

Dark and light

Season: Advent

General introduction to the theme

The Bible tells us that God is light and doesn't have any darkness in him (1 John 1:5). This light is both the first gift of creation (Genesis 1:3) and the abiding reality of the new creation (Revelation 21:23). God's light has never stopped shining and is reflected in the lives of individuals such as Moses, Deborah, Elijah, Isaiah and Paul. It shines most clearly in Jesus, who is the light that shines in the darkness and the true light that the darkness has never put out (John 1:5, 9). In the Gospels we read how Jesus shines his light into the lives of the people he touches and how he once gave his followers a glimpse of the glory of God's light at the transfiguration. The light of Jesus reveals God and dispels all darkness, disarming it by the cross and resurrection. The story of the Bible is the triumph of light over dark for all who put their trust in Jesus, who brings us out of darkness into his marvellous light (1 Peter 2:9).

Reflective overview

You will need:

A Bible, a large circle of grey felt with a hole at the centre, three large candles, several small craft mirror pieces (with a non-reflective side), six large craft mirror pieces, six wooden hearts, a round piece of shiny reflective material (the same size and shape as the grey felt), a candle snuffer and matches.

Bible story: Genesis 1:1–2

Action: *Open up the Bible and then lay it down at your side.*

Script: God has given us the stories in his book that show us what he is like.

Action: *Place down the three candles and light them.*

Script: God is light and doesn't have any darkness in him.

Action: *Lay out the circle of grey felt around the candles.*

Script: In the beginning, God created the heavens and the earth. The earth was empty and with no form of life—but the Spirit of God was there.

Bible story: Genesis 1:3

Action: *Place the small pieces of mirror all over the grey felt, reflective side up.*

Script: God who is light said, 'I command light to shine!' … and there was light.

Bible story: John 3:19–20

Action: *Turn over some of the mirror pieces and move them away from the flames.*

Script: But people turned away from the light.

Bible story: Exodus 2—40

Action: *Place a large mirror piece down. Place a wooden heart on it.*

Script: There was a person who loved God and reflected the light. His name was Moses. Moses listened to God's word and shone the light to God's people through dark times in the desert.

Bible story: Judges 4—5

Action: *Place a large mirror piece down. Place a wooden heart on it.*

Script: There was a person who loved God and reflected the light. Her name was Deborah. Deborah listened to God's word and shone the light to God's people through dark times of fighting.

Bible story: 1 Kings 17 to 2 Kings 2

Action: *Place a large mirror piece down. Place a wooden heart on it.*

Script: There was a person who loved God and reflected the light. His name was Elijah. Elijah listened to God's word and shone the light to God's people through dark times when they ignored him.

Bible story: Isaiah 1—11

Action: *Place a large mirror piece down. Place a wooden heart on it.*

Script: There was a person who loved God and reflected the light. His name was Isaiah. Isaiah listened to God's word and he shone the light to God's people, showing the future to those who walked in darkness.

Bible story: John 8:12; John 18—21

Action: *Remove one of the candles from the middle and place it on the grey felt.*

Script: There was a person who was God and was the light. His name was Jesus. Jesus said, 'I am the light for the world! Follow me, and you won't be walking in the dark. You will have the light that gives life.'

Jesus took that light into the deepest darkness…

Action: *With a snuffer, extinguish the flame of the candle on the grey felt. Then pause before relighting it with a match lit from one of the central candles still burning.*

Script: But God brought his light back to life again. The light of Jesus shines in the darkness and the darkness has not overcome it.

Action: *Pause again before returning the 'Jesus candle' back to the centre.*

Bible story: Acts 9—28

Action: *Place a large mirror piece down. Place a wooden heart on it.*

Script: There was a person who loved God and reflected the light. His name was Paul. Paul listened to God's word and he shone the light to many people in many countries.

Bible story: Revelation 22:5

Action: *Place a large mirror piece down. Place a wooden heart on it.*

Script: I wonder…
How we reflect the light…
What things we choose to do that reflect the light…
What parts of who we are reflect the light…
Who we reflect the light to…

Action: *Carefully move the three candles to the side and place the shiny fabric over the grey felt. Put all three candles back into the centre.*

Script: There will be a time when everyone will walk in the light. There will be no darkness, no need for lamps or sun. For God, who is light, will shine everywhere.
I wonder…
What that will be like…
How we will reflect the light then…

Sinai shining
The story of Moses

Bible links

Exodus 33 and 34

You will need:

Kitchen foil, fluorescent paper, silver card, small craft mirrors, a torch, various versions of Exodus 34:6, large piece of card

— The Barnabas Children's Bible —

Stories 45—66

Background to the story

Moses was chosen by God to reflect God's light to the people of Israel and lead them out of slavery. He encountered God's light in the burning bush in the desert; he followed God's light in the bright cloud that went before the people as they escaped from Egypt; he witnessed the majesty of God's light in the fire and lightning that surrounded Mount Sinai. It was within the heart of this 'shekinah' glory on the mountain that God spoke to Moses to give him the Ten Commandments and the pattern for making the tabernacle. Moses was also given a glimpse of God's glorious light. As God passed in front of Moses, he said, 'I am the Lord God. I am merciful and very patient with my people. I show great love, and I can be trusted' (Exodus 34:6). It was following this second mountain-top experience that Moses most clearly began to reflect God's light. Everyone saw that his face shone because he had been talking with God (v. 29).

Open the story

Use the following warm-up idea, with plenty of mime and actions, as a way of retelling the story up to the moment when God asked Moses to climb Mount Sinai for the second time.

When Moses was born *(rock a child in your arms)*, the Pharaoh of Egypt wanted to kill all the baby boys *(hide the baby in terror)*. Moses was hidden in the bulrushes along the River Nile *(crouch down low, hiding the baby)*, but was found by Pharaoh's daughter, who decided to keep him *(lift the baby up high)*. Moses grew up in the Pharaoh's court *(dance like an Egyptian)*, but he never forgot that he was really a Hebrew child *(dance to a Jewish rhythm: step to the left 1, clap 2, step to the right 1, clap 2, as in the rhythm of the chorus 'Jesus put this song into my heart')*.

One day, when Moses saw his people being treated badly, he fought and killed an Egyptian guard *(conduct a mock fight)*. He then had to run for his life *(run hard on the spot)*. Moses became a shepherd in the land of Midian *(start counting sheep; add in some sheep noises)*. One day he saw a bush on fire *(shade your eyes and look intently at an imaginary bush)*. It was shining with a light that did not dim *(shield your eyes)*. Moses took off his shoes and approached the light *(mime this action, tiptoeing carefully on the spot)*. God spoke to him and gave him the job of leading his people to freedom *(make a shocked face)*. God promised Moses that he would help him *(make a scared face)*.

Moses went to Pharaoh and said 'Let my people go' *(stamp one foot on the ground)*. The Pharaoh refused again and again *(turn around with folded arms)*. Then many strange and terrible things started to happen in the land of Egypt *(briefly mime your way through the plagues with actions for tasting blood in the water, dodging hopping frogs, swatting flies, making animal noises, scratching boils, killing gnats, swiping at buzzing locusts, groping in the dark, dodging hailstones, and weeping for dead sons)*. Finally, Pharaoh let the people go and Moses led them to freedom *(march off with determination)*. But Pharaoh changed his mind *(run faster and faster)*. The people were trapped by the Sea of Reeds, but God opened up a way to go *(walk gingerly across a muddy sea bed)*. They arrived safely on the other side and were free *(jump for joy)*.

Moses led the people through the desert *(tramp, tramp)*. The people grumbled but God provided them with water from the rock *(gulp, gulp)*, and food for each day *(munch, munch)*. Finally they arrived at Mount Sinai *(look up in awe)*. God's holy mountain was ablaze with light *(shield eyes)*. Only Moses went up the mountain, and was away for 40 days and 40 nights *(tap watch)*. The people thought he'd gone missing, so they decided to make a golden calf to worship *(all bow down)*. Suddenly, Moses appeared. He was really angry *(look angry)*. He smashed the Ten Commandments he had brought down the mountain *(smash, smash)* and he felt like giving up as the people's leader *(look fed up)*. But God called him up the mountain again *(climbing actions)* and this is what happened next…

Tell the story

Moses' second mountain-top experience was truly amazing! Tell the story, ensuring that the children become part of it as it unfolds—for example, being awestruck at the idea of talking with God; becoming puzzled about what to do next; hiding in the cleft of the rock; being dazzled by the glorious light of God; writing out the Ten Commandments; reacting to the shining face of Moses. The key points to the story can be found in Exodus 33:1—34:33 as follows.

* God tells Moses to go on with the people but without God's presence (33:1–3).
* God often speaks to Moses at the 'meeting tent', 'face to face, just like a friend' (Exodus 33:11).
* Moses decides to continue with the work and wants God to bring them all to the new land (33:13).
* God promises to go with them (33:14).
* God says he will let Moses see his glory (33:19–23).
* God calls Moses up the mountain for a second time (34:2).
* Moses catches a fleeting glimpse of God. God reminds Moses (and us!) how amazing God is (34:6).
* Moses writes out the Ten Commandments for a second time (34:27–28).
* Moses comes back down the mountain with his face shining brightly because God has been speaking to him (34:29).
* Moses has to put a veil over his face, because it is shining so brightly (34:33).

Talk about the story

Moses had already given so much of himself that he must have truly despaired when the people forgot God so easily. God had been faithful in bringing them safely out of Egypt, taking them across the desert and showing them the way to go. But still they turned to other gods instead. Why might this have happened? What might Moses have thought about it all? Does this sort of thing happen today? What does God feel like when people so easily forget all the good things that he does for them?

Wonder together about what it would be like to meet God in the way that Moses did. What might it feel like? What might God look like, even if only from the back, as Moses saw him? Talk about what the children would say to God if they could talk with him in the way that Moses did. What questions would they ask? What thoughts would go through their minds?

With older children, you might like to read 2 Corinthians 3:7–18, where Paul uses this very story to help us into the truth that, because of Jesus, we can all now reflect God's true light as Moses did. As we reflect that light, it also changes us to become more and more like Jesus. Talk about how this can happen. Have the children ever met people who seem to shine with God's goodness and presence?

Play with the story

As a craft activity, focus on the different ways in which light is reflected throughout Moses' story: first from the bush, then from the cloud, then on the mountain and finally from Moses' face. Cut out shapes for each of the items and cover them with various reflective materials, such as kitchen foil, fluorescent paper, silver card, and so on. Finally, for Moses' face, use small mirror pieces from a craft shop, such as the ones used in the reflective overview (see page 30).

Now shine a bright torchlight on to the different objects to reproduce what happened in the story. Explain that the bright light represents God and each of the objects and people reflect that light.

Attach the various objects to a bigger piece of card to act as an overall visual for the story.

Reflect on the story

Read Exodus 34:6 in different Bible versions and choose the one you like best. Print out the verse and mount each part on a separate piece of card. Use the cards as a focus for your prayers. For example (using words from the RSV):

* God's grace and mercy: ask for help both to express and to receive mercy in our day-to-day lives.
* God's slowness to anger: think about times when we get angry too quickly and for the wrong reasons.

- God's steadfast love: think about people who especially need to know God's unchanging love at this time.
- God's faithfulness: think about our own commitment to stay true to God in the week ahead.

Deborah's day

The story of Deborah and Barak

Bible links

Judges 4 and 5

You will need:

Cards showing names of Bible women and brief descriptions, silver card and craft materials to decorate shields, iron filings and a magnet

— The Barnabas Children's Bible —

Story 88

Background to the story

Deborah's story is set during the years when the people of Israel were settling in to the promised land but were under constant harassment and attack from the tribes who were living in Canaan at that time. God chose a succession of judges to give wise leadership to God's people, to inspire them to put their faith in God and not be tempted to throw their lot in with the Canaanites, who believed in many gods.

Deborah was the first and only woman judge, and she was also a prophet (Judges 4:4). She was known for her wise decisions and was respected by the people. She saw how they were being oppressed by King Jabin, through his military commander Sisera, so she appealed to Barak to lead soldiers from the northern tribes of Zebulun and Naphtali to respond to this aggression and deal with Sisera and his army. Barak held Deborah in such high regard that he would not go to battle without her. Deborah made it clear that the victory would be God's alone (Judges 4:9).

God helped Deborah and Barak to win a great victory: it seems that the Canaanite chariots got stuck in the mud when the Kishon River broke its banks (see Judges 5:21). Sisera ran for his life but was killed by another woman, Jael, in the very place where he sought sanctuary.

Deborah and Barak sing a song of praise to God in Judges 5. This is a very ancient poem and is a victory song that tells how God marches with his people, stirs them up again and again to fight enemies, and helps them in their wars. It includes a very moving description of how Sisera's mother waited in vain for her son's return: this is the sad hidden cost of all such wars. It ends with a blessing on the Lord's people, who, like Deborah, are to shine with light, like the sun at its brightest (Judges 5:31).

Open the story

So many of the Old Testament stories are dominated by male role models that it is important to include stories such as Deborah's, which is a rare but welcome celebration of the role of women among those who reflect God's light. Deborah's light shines brightly: she is the only judge who is also a prophet and she is counted among the military commanders of God's people, as well as being, in her own words, 'a mother' to Israel (Judges 5:7).

To remind the children of some of the stories of women in the Bible, play a game in which you hide a number of names of Bible women and then, on separate pieces of card, some of the reasons for which they are well known. Encourage the children to find the women and match them up with the reasons why they are famous.

- Eve: mother of all who live (Genesis 3:20)
- Sarah: example of hope, obedience and holy living (1 Peter 3:5–6)
- Rebekah: example of courage (Genesis 24:57–58)
- Rahab: rescuer of the spies in Jericho (Joshua 2:15)
- Ruth: loyal daughter-in-law and ancestor to King David (the book of Ruth)
- Miriam: prophetess and dancer (Exodus 15:20)
- Huldah: prophetess (2 Kings 22:14)
- Esther: brave queen (the book of Esther)
- Mary: the mother of Jesus (Luke 1:26–38; 2:5–7)
- Anna: prophetess who became one of the first evangelists (Luke 2:36–38)
- Mary Magdalene: first person to see Jesus alive after the resurrection (John 20:10–18)

- Philip's four daughters: all prophetesses! (Acts 21:8–9)
- Priscilla: teacher and friend of Paul (Acts 18:2, 26)
- Phoebe: church leader (Romans 16:1)

Another way to set the scene for today's story would be to put the girls in charge of things for the session. Let them give instructions to the others, answer all the questions and make all the decisions.

Tell the story

As you tell the story, ask the children to create some of the objects you mention by linking up and becoming human statues of each of the following items.

- The seat on which Deborah sits as judge.
- One or more of the iron chariots that Sisera commanded.
- Mount Tabor, near which the battle took place.
- Some of the weapons that were used in the battle: for example a shield, a sword and a spear.
- The river Kishon, which flows through the valley.
- Sisera's chariot, stuck in the mud and abandoned.
- The tent in which Sisera hid.
- The instruments to which Deborah and Barak sang their victory song (choose your own instruments).

Talk about the story

Alongside her many attributes, Deborah was also a good singer and songwriter. Create an acrostic poem that tells the story of Deborah and Barak (each line starting with a letter of each of their names). For example:

Dark days had come upon the people of God.
Enemies such as Jabin ruled them with an iron rod,
But God chose Deborah to be in command.
On her special seat she judged the land,
Ruling what was right over what was wrong,
Always listening to God's own song.
Her bravery defeated proud Sisera and his men.

Alternatively, make up a song like Deborah's. Use the tune of a well-known nursery rhyme with a military flavour such as 'The Grand Old Duke of York'.

Here is an example of how it might sound, celebrating this Bible story. Can you add more verses?

Deborah and Barak,
They had 10,000 men,
They marched them up to Mount Tabor
And they marched them back again.
And when they were there, they won,
And when they had won, they sang,
And when the people heard their song
They knew what God had done.

Play with the story

Deborah's words of encouragement to Barak are key to the story and an insight into her amazing faith in God: 'Today the Lord is going to help you… In fact, the Lord has already gone on ahead to fight for you' (Judges 4:14). God promises to go before us into all situations. Jesus promises something similar to his disciples in Matthew 28:20.

As a craft activity, make a shield, like one that Deborah and Barak might have taken into battle, and design a crest for the shield that includes some of Deborah's words. Use some shiny material to make the shield so that it will reflect the light and pick up the theme at the end of Deborah's song, where she sings that the people of God will shine like the sun (Judges 5:31).

Reflect on the story

Collect some iron filings and place them on a flat surface under which you can manoeuvre a magnet. Remind the children that Sisera's army had iron chariots. These represented a powerful technological advance on anything that Barak and Deborah could muster, but God made up the difference. Talk about some of the big and daunting challenges that the children might be facing at the moment. As each one is mentioned, move some of the iron filings to the edge by the invisible force of the magnet. This is a symbol of how God's invisible power is available to help us and go ahead of us into every situation. Each time you do this, say together some words linked to Deborah's encouragement to Barak, such as 'Thank you, Lord, that you have gone ahead of us to help us.'

Mountain a challenge
The story of Elijah

Bible links

1 Kings 17—19

You will need:

The Incredibles DVD and player (optional), a digital camera, paper, crayons, safety scissors

— The Barnabas Children's Bible —

Stories 162—169

Background to the story

Elijah was chosen to shine for God in his generation, challenging the godless influence that Queen Jezebel held over both her husband King Ahab and the people of Israel. It is never easy to be a prophet: Elijah was even forced to leave his homeland because of the threats to his life that came because he spoke the truth. Elijah had declared that there would be a three-year drought in the land but, at the end of this time, 'the biggest troublemaker in Israel' (as Ahab calls Elijah in 1 Kings 18:17) returned to challenge the priests of the false gods (the Baals) to a contest on Mount Carmel. 'The one who answers by starting the fire is God,' said Elijah (18:24). There followed an extraordinarily dramatic story of what happened on the mountain that day. Elijah knew that the Lord is the true God and that his powerful light will win the day, scattering the darkness of what is evil.

Open the story

Ask the children to stand in a circle, facing outwards. On the count of three, they should all turn and become statues of whichever character or mood the leader has stipulated. Use the following words and ideas: Mr Incredible; depressed; Superman; lonely; Elastigirl; doubtful; Violet; despairing; Dash; hopeless. If you prefer, you could play charades with the superheroes' names instead.

Show the clip from *The Incredibles* where Bob/ Mr Incredible has a terrible day at work, comes home and the car falls apart, or talk about the way even Mr Incredible has his ups and downs in the film.

Tell the story

Introduce Elijah—a he-man of a prophet who was trying to be faithful to God at a time when the king (Ahab) was a mean, cowardly tyrant married to a woman called Jezebel. Jezebel openly worshipped other gods such as Baal and Asherah, and was making the people of God worship them, too.

Working in pairs or threes, give the children one or more sections of the story, either from Bibles or from the summary below. Ask them to make a 'freeze frame' (a frozen camera moment) of a part of their section that they think is important. Ask each group in turn to make their freeze frame. You then tell the story from what you see in the frames.

Story summary

King Ahab and his queen, Jezebel, did such terrible things that God's prophet Elijah told them no rain would fall unless he commanded it. Then Elijah went into hiding near Cherith Brook, where God sent ravens to bring him bread and meat every day.

When the Cherith Brook dried up, God sent Elijah to a widow in a town called Zarephath. The widow was baking her last loaf of bread: she thought that she and her son would then die of hunger. But Elijah asked her to make him a loaf, too, and promised her that her flour and oil would never run out during the drought. And that's what happened!

The widow's son then became ill and died. The widow was sad and angry with Elijah for letting her son die. But Elijah prayed and the boy came back to life again.

After three years of no rain, God sent Elijah to meet King Ahab and to challenge the priests of Baal to a showdown on Mount Carmel to see whose god was the true god. The 450 priests of Baal killed a bull, put the meat on a pile of wood, and then prayed to Baal to light the altar. They prayed all afternoon, but nothing happened. Elijah made fun of them and they prayed louder until teatime, but still nothing happened.

Then Elijah built an altar, piled it up with wood, dug a trench round it, killed a bull, put the meat on top and then poured gallons and gallons of water over the whole thing until the water ran into the trench. Elijah prayed, asking God to prove that he was the God of Abraham, Isaac and Jacob, so that the people would change their minds and follow him again. Straight away a fire came from heaven and burnt up everything—even the stones of the altar. Everyone cried out, 'The Lord is God!' and Elijah went into the valley of Kishon and killed all the priests of Baal.

Elijah climbed back up Mount Carmel and saw the rain coming at last. He told Ahab to ride home in his chariot before he got wet. Elijah was so full of the Holy Spirit that he ran ahead of the chariot all the way back to the palace in Jezreel.

Queen Jezebel heard that Elijah had killed all her priests and swore to kill him, too, but Elijah ran away. He walked into the desert for a day and then sat down under a bush. Elijah told God that he was no good, that he'd had enough and that he wanted to die. An angel brought him bread and water and he slept, but the angel told him he needed to carry on with his journey. Elijah walked for 40 days and nights to Mount Sinai, where he hid in a cave.

Elijah was hiding in the cave when he heard God ask him, 'Elijah, why are you here?' Elijah told God he'd done his best but that he was scared of being killed. God told Elijah to go and stand in front of the cave and he would pass by him. There was a roaring wind, which was so strong that it shattered rocks, but God wasn't in the wind. There was a massive earthquake, but God wasn't in the earthquake. There was a fire, but God wasn't in the fire. Finally, there was a gentle breeze and God spoke to Elijah again. Then God gave Elijah another job to do, so that God's work could carry on.

Talk about the story

Talk about which of all the scenes shows Elijah at a high point—the most heroic moment in his work for God. Invite someone to become Elijah in the 'hot seat' and have the others ask him or her questions to find out how Elijah might have been feeling and thinking. Which was the lowest point for Elijah? Again, invite someone to be Elijah in the hot seat and have the others find out how Elijah might have been feeling

and thinking. (In hot seating, someone sits on a chair and becomes a different character. The others ask her or him questions to try to discover something about the character. The person answers as if they are that character. It's not a guessing game; it's a framework to get to know a character better.)

Alternatively, talk about Elijah's story with some open-ended questions. For example:

* I wonder what surprises you about this story…
* I wonder what puzzles you about this story…
* I wonder if you've ever felt like Elijah when he was alone by the brook… facing the king… on Mount Carmel… on the run from Jezebel…
* I wonder why Elijah felt so low after he had been so high…
* I wonder when God loved him most…
* I wonder if God only loves us when we're doing things for him…

Play with the story

* As a group, draw a map with cartoon scenes of the events of the story and arrows leading from one to the other.
* Re-form the freeze frames from earlier and, using a digital camera, make a photo story of Elijah's life with captions.

Reflect on the story

In the New Testament, Elijah is held up as a hero of faith, especially for the power of his prayer life (James 5:17). He is also one of the two figures who appeared with Jesus at the transfiguration, standing as a representative of all the Old Testament prophets (Matthew 17:1–8).

Ask the children to draw round their hand and cut out the outline. In the outline, invite them to write one word or draw a picture of the one thing that they want to go on praying about in the week ahead. Ask them to hold on to the prayer hands in silence for a short while before laying them down in such a way as to create the outline of a mountain. This can remind them both of the place where God answered Elijah by fire (at Carmel) and of God's answer in the gentle breeze at Sinai (also known as Horeb). Encourage the children to listen out for how God will answer their prayers, whether quietly or very dramatically, as in the story of Elijah.

A light in dark times
The story of Isaiah's vision

Bible links

Isaiah 6:1—9:7

You will need:

Objects for sound effects (such as a large 'wobble board'), kitchen foil, pieces of white fabric, a long piece of gold-coloured fabric, a CD of heavenly music, craft materials, tissue paper (in black, yellow, red and orange), a plant pot with a small sprouting shoot

— The Barnabas Children's Bible —

Story 194

Background to the story

Isaiah lived in times that were precarious for God's people. The kingdom had split in two and there was rivalry between the tribes of Israel in the north and Judah in the south. Furthermore, there were dangerous forces at work abroad, as the power of the Assyrians in the east was on the increase. The Assyrian nation was the up-and-coming empire, and little kingdoms such as Israel or Judah could be easily swallowed up or end up in the no-man's-land between Egypt and Assyria. Into this situation Isaiah was called to shine for God. He had to remind the people to serve the true Lord and not be tempted to turn to other alternative gods or rely on their own strength.

Being a prophet is never easy, and Isaiah tells the story of how God chose him to do this job, with frankness and honesty (Isaiah 6:1–8). Isaiah had an amazing experience of God's presence that dramatically changed his life and must have sustained him through the dark times that lay ahead. He never forgot the bright vision of heaven that he was asked to reflect in his day and age.

Isaiah's work as a prophet spanned the reigns of four kings, some of whom were very hostile to God indeed. To each one, he spoke God's message of judgment and hope and, in particular, he proclaimed the promise of the great light that one day would come for those who walked in darkness (Isaiah 9:2).

Open the story

Talk about the most exciting and the most frightening experiences that the children have had to face. The conversation may touch on dramatic thunderstorms, scary fairground rides or seeing some amazing natural phenomena such as shooting stars. Make sure you share your experiences, too. Explore how they felt, what difference the experiences made and how they will remember them in future—or would they rather forget them? Link the conversation to the amazing experience that Isaiah tells us about in today's Bible story.

Tell the story

Create some sound effects and atmosphere with the following items for the children to use as you tell the story from Isaiah 6:1–8.

- A large piece of stiff card that, when wobbled, sounds like thunder.
- A large sheet of kitchen foil that, when shaken, makes its own distinct sound and sparkles.
- A boiling kettle to create some steam like the smoke in the story.
- Six pieces of white sheeting that can be flapped to represent the wings of the angels.
- A large bright yellow or gold-coloured cloth, held at the four corners to represent the robe that filled the temple.
- Some heavenly music such as Thomas Tallis's *Spem in alium*, to catch the atmosphere of the angels' song.
- An electric fire with artificial coals to represent the place from which the burning coal was taken (take care that it is only the light that is on, not any of the electric bars).

Build up the atmosphere of the story with all the sound effects and visuals. Also, explore some of the feelings that Isaiah must have gone through, by asking the children to adopt expressions of sadness, shock, amazement, horror, guilt, excitement and so on.

Talk about the story

What might Isaiah have felt the day (or week) after his experience? Invite the children to step into Isaiah's trembling shoes and imagine what he might have said to his family or friends about what happened on that day. What might he have thought about it all afterwards? Would he have worked out what it all meant? Why might God have chosen to speak to Isaiah so dramatically?

Isaiah now had a difficult job before him. King Ahaz was especially wicked according to the stories (you can read about some of his deeds in 2 Chronicles 28), but Isaiah was told to speak to him, challenging him to put his trust in God and telling him some home truths about his behaviour. Isaiah had to reflect God's light into some very dark places, but God had prepared him for the fact that, very often, people would not listen to what he had to say (see Isaiah 6:9–12).

How do we persuade someone to change their mind? What ways work best? What has anyone tried that has worked? What might have worked for Isaiah, who had to talk King Ahaz into changing his mind about God?

Play with the story

According to the story, the seraphim are six-winged angels. What might they have looked like? Invite the children to create their own pictures of how they imagine the angels.

The burning coal that the angel picked up with tongs from the fire is often used as a symbol for Isaiah. The coal touched his lips and brought him forgiveness. In this sense, it has often been likened to the gift of forgiveness that Jesus brings because of the cross. Make the burning coal by scrunching up some black tissue paper into a tight ball and then attaching, with clear tape, some small pieces of bunched-up yellow, orange and red wool to be like the glowing embers.

The burning coal is a picture of being accepted by God: 'Your sins are forgiven, and you are no longer guilty' (Isaiah 6:7). Isaiah no longer needed to fear being in God's presence. For him, the burning coal became a sign of God's love and welcome. It is as if God was saying to him, 'I love you and I want you to speak for me.' Ask the children to attach the coals they have made to their pictures of the amazing angel and invite them to write their own version of Isaiah 6:7 on the finished picture.

Reflect on the story

Isaiah had had a glimpse of the glorious light of heaven, which he now needed to reflect on earth. The message he had to share wasn't an easy one but it did contain hope. Even though the people would eventually be defeated and taken into exile, there would still be a 'stump' left—the part of the tree left in the ground when it has been felled. It is from this stump that the holy seed would come. God promises this in Isaiah 6:13, and the image comes again in Isaiah 11:1.

As a picture of the hope God gave to Isaiah, bring in a tiny seedling growing in a pot. Talk about situations that seem hard and hopeless in the world and in the children's own experience and, as a way of putting his or her trust in God, encourage each child in turn to pick up the plant pot at some stage in the conversation. Finally, say together, 'Thank you, Lord, that you give us hope.'

Approachable light
The story of Jesus

Bible links

John 1:9, 14; John 8:12; John 12:35–36

You will need:

Various light bulbs, candles and other sources of light, a projected light, blindfolds, yellow and black paper, paints, an icon of the transfiguration, large versions of John 8:12 to decorate and colour, eight stand-alone candles

— The Barnabas Children's Bible —

Stories 247 to 252 (the birth of Jesus); Story 291 (Bartimaeus); Story 278 (the transfiguration)

Background to the story

Jesus reflected most perfectly the light of God: 'God's Son has all the brightness of God's own glory and is like him in every way' (Hebrews 1:3). He was the approachable light of God for us on earth, enabling us to come close to God, who 'created all the lights in the heavens' (James 1:17), and the one who otherwise 'lives in light that no one can come near' (1 Timothy 6:16). Jesus shows us God and calls himself the light for the world. This is the light that enters into the deep darkness of Easter and emerges triumphant, enabling us to become the children of light we were always meant to be. From the little light in the hay in the Bethlehem stable, through the dazzling light at the transfiguration, to the light of the resurrection morning, Jesus has reflected for us the light of heaven on earth. The story focuses on different aspects of Jesus' life, especially his birth, miracles of healing and transfiguration.

Open the story

Compare the brightness of different sorts of light, including the light from a match, a candle, a torch, 40, 60, 80 and 100 watt bulbs and a flash bulb. Intensity of light is measured in lumens (*lumen* is the Latin word for 'light').

Ask the children to think about how much brighter the sun's light appears than any of the other stars that we can see in the universe. Explain that all of God's light reflected in the lives of his people is like these lesser lights compared to the full-blown light of God revealed in Jesus.

We also use the word 'light' in another sense, meaning something not heavy but easy to carry. Jesus is the full-blown brightness of God's light, but when he came to earth he did not blind us with that light; we were able to bear it. Jesus is God's approachable light. Do some of the following light-related activities.

- Project a light on to a wall and then introduce a variety of silhouettes of different objects and animals. You could even cut out an outline from a photograph of someone the children might know. Can they guess what or who each silhouette is from? God's light in Jesus shows up what we are truly like.
- Challenge the children to accomplish certain tasks wearing blindfolds so that they cannot see what they are doing. Then allow them to do the task again, but this time with guidance from a friend who can see. God's light in Jesus helps us to find the way in life.
- Divide into teams and play a picture-guessing game, where one person at a time from each team goes to the leader to be told a light-related word, which they must then go back to draw for the others to guess.
- Create some group sculptures of different light-related objects.

Tell the story

In this section, there are three stories and linked activities. Divide into three groups and work on the activities below to explore ways in which Jesus shows us that he is the light for the world.

1. God turned on the brightness of his approachable light when Jesus was born in this world. In one of the prophecies from the book of Isaiah, we read what this arrival will be like: 'Jerusalem, stand up! Shine! Your new day is dawning. The glory of the Lord shines brightly on you. The earth and its people are covered with darkness, but the glory of the Lord is shining upon you. Nations and kings will come to the light of your dawning day' (Isaiah 60:1–3). This light was first sung about on the hillside by the angels, then seen in the hay of the manger by the shepherds and also treasured in the hearts of Mary and Joseph. Create a group collage to explore the light of Christmas by using bright yellow and black paper or yellow and black paints to illustrate the following:

- The sun breaking out over the horizon.
- The bright lights of the angelic choir on the hillside.
- The glow from the stable in the back streets of Bethlehem.
- The breaking out of light in many places on a dark circle of the earth.

2. Jesus shone light into the lives of the people he met, bringing them healing, hope and wholeness. Perhaps the best illustration of how people met with the light is seen in the stories of Jesus healing those who were blind. Read together the story of the blind beggar in Luke 18:35–43. (The beggar is named as Bartimaeus in Mark 10:46.) It's a great story to act out, with Bartimaeus' loud shouts, the busy crowds milling around Jesus, the annoyed reactions of some of the people (including, probably, the disciples), Jesus' own words to Bartimaeus, and the excitement of the healing. Invite the children to step into the story and capture the amazement of God's light opening up blind eyes.

3. There was one moment when Jesus allowed three of his followers to catch a glimpse of the true brightness of his light. It happened at the transfiguration (Luke 9:28–36). Peter, James and John were overawed by the brightness of the light shining through Jesus. For a moment, Jesus could be seen standing with Moses and Elijah, both of whom, in their time, had also shone with God's light. Print an icon of the transfiguration from the internet and talk about the way the event has been depicted. There are no shadows in icons. Instead, the light shines out from Jesus to enlighten everything and everybody. It was such a special event that Jesus told his disciples not to talk about it until after the resurrection. Peter never forgot the experience (2 Peter 1:17–18).

Talk about the story

Looking back on the three stories above, which story did the children like best? Which one did they think was the most important? Which one showed them most about who Jesus is? Which other stories about Jesus also show us God's light touching people's lives?

Play with the story

A key verse for the stories is John 8:12. Print out the verse in large block letters and provide coloured pens and craft materials for the children to interpret the words of the verse.

Reflect on the story

God's light in Jesus had to 'go out' for a while (see John 12:35–36) as he plunged into the darkest places of suffering and death on the cross on Good Friday. To end the session and give an opportunity for reflection, light a series of seven candles and then extinguish them one by one, as you briefly outline each part of the Good Friday story.

1. Jesus was betrayed.
2. Jesus was put on trial.
3. Jesus was mocked.
4. Jesus was tortured.
5. Jesus was condemned to death.
6. Jesus was put on a cross.
7. Jesus died.

Pause after extinguishing each candle. Watch the smoke drift off slowly and give space for reflection. Finally, say, 'But Jesus' light is stronger than death.' Produce a new candle. Reposition the seven candles in a circle and place the new candle in the middle. At the beginning of the new creation (known as the eighth day), Jesus' light came back to us for ever.

Blinding light
The story of Paul's conversion

Bible links

Acts 9:1–31; Acts 22 and 26

You will need:

The number cards from a pack of cards, paper for the battleships game, parchment paper for the craft, a camera with a flash, a set of arrow outlines

— The Barnabas Children's Bible —

Story 326

Background to the story

It is hard to imagine a greater turnaround than Saul's conversion. When God's light shone into his life, it quite literally knocked Saul for six. When he met Jesus on the road to Damascus, he was on his way to arrest Christians, so convinced was he that they had got everything wrong. Three days later, he was absolutely certain that Jesus was the Son of God, and he was prepared to stand up and tell his fellow persecutors that it was they who had got it all wrong. No wonder the Christians back in Jerusalem found it hard to accept that Saul was now one of them. Perhaps God's light had to shine so dramatically for Saul because he was destined to reflect so much of that light in his missionary work around the Mediterranean. Saul, who later used his Roman name Paul, could not forget the day Jesus appeared to him. In fact, it seems that he must have often spoken about it when preaching the gospel; we have two accounts of what happened in Acts 22 and 26, where he tells his amazing story.

Open the story

Saul was a very devout Pharisee. To him, the claim of the 'followers of the Way' (as the Christians were called then) that Jesus was God's Son was pure heresy—the worst sort of lie. You couldn't have found anyone more determined to stamp out Christianity. The context of the story is that most Christians were running for cover, in fear of their lives. Play some simple hide-and-seek games to pick up on the story. Either hide some small objects that the children have to find, or, if you have the space, play a proper game of hide-and-seek.

To illustrate Saul's hunt for the groups of Christians hiding in Damascus, play a game of pairs. Using just the number cards from a pack of cards, place the cards face down on a large table. How many same-suit or same-number pairs can each child find?

Alternatively, play an adapted version of the game of battleships. Divide the children into two teams, each one with a 10 x 10 grid, numbered across the top and with letters down the side. Explain that the grid represents the streets of Damascus. Each team secretly hides five sets of Christians together somewhere on the grid—two or three Christians in adjacent squares. Each team in turn now tries to guess in which squares the Christians are hiding: is it A1 or B7 (and so on)? Which team of Pharisees from Jerusalem can find and arrest all the other team's Christians first?

Tell the story

Step into the story of Saul's visit to Damascus. Give some background to the story and then divide the children into two groups, one of which becomes the soldiers with Saul on the way to Damascus and the other a band of Christians hiding in the city. Give each group time to discuss the following questions:

- What sort of things will they be talking about together?
- What do they think will happen in the next couple of days?
- What are their main worries or hopes?
- What secret things are they thinking about?

Share the children's thoughts and then build on what they have said by telling the story of what happened next (Acts 9:10–16).

Ananias was certainly a very brave man! There are all sorts of reasons why he could have perhaps ignored the vision he had. Set up a 'conscience alley', in which half the group urge Ananias not to go to see Saul and the other half urge him to go. Whose arguments will win the day?

What might have been going through Saul's mind during those three days when he could not see? The light had been so bright that it had blinded him. When he did see again, everything looked different! Those who were once enemies, Saul now saw as his brothers and sisters, and his former friends were now out to kill him. Saul now knew that Jesus, who previously had seemed like an impostor and a fraud, was the Son of God. Saul's life had been turned upside down.

Pick up on the change in Saul from one extreme to another. In a circle, play a word game in which one child says an adjective (a describing word) and another child has to come up with an adjective that means the opposite. Alternatively, play a back-to-front game in which a leader spells certain words slowly backwards (perhaps words that appear in the story). Who can spot the real word first?

Talk about the story

The story of Saul's conversion is so well known that the phrase 'a Damascus road experience' is often used to describe a complete change of heart and mind about something. However, it is important to recognise that Saul did not simply have a rethink about life. He really did see God's light and hear Jesus' voice. Saul's story was so remarkable that Ananias had heard something about it (see Acts 9:17) and later Barnabas also had heard it (see v. 27).

Ask the children to imagine that they're working on the reporting team for the *Damascus Daily*. They've been sent to interview Saul after his experience. They need to work out what sort of probing questions they would like to ask Saul. What sort of story will they write up for the newspaper? What will be their eye-catching headline?

Play with the story

Saul's escape over the walls of the city is quite comical, although in reality it was very serious. It's now Saul's life that is in danger. Act out the story, working up scenes linked to the events in Acts 9:23–25:

- Sneaking through the Damascus streets, dodging the religious police.
- Climbing up the walls.
- Sorting out the ropes and the basket.
- Saying goodbye and giving some last words of advice.
- Lowering the basket down precariously.

Talk about what happened after Saul had disappeared into the night. Might he have felt relief, sadness or fear? Ask the children to imagine they are from Damascus and discover the empty basket lying at the bottom of the wall the next day. In it they discover a short farewell note written by Saul. Recreate the imaginary note and make it look like a piece of parchment from long ago that is now a museum piece. Perhaps it is torn, slightly crumpled and going brown at the edges. Saul would have had to write his words of farewell in a hurry.

Reflect on the story

Read Acts 9:3: 'A bright light from heaven suddenly flashed around him.' After Saul's experience, he reflected Jesus' light to many people and in many places in the years that followed. Have available a camera with a flash and some large arrow outlines. Gather in a circle and put the arrows together, all facing the same way, in the middle of the circle. God's light meant that Saul's life was turned around and he saw things differently. Talk about the things that the children would like to see changed in the world. What new beginnings do they hope for? What dead ends have they experienced that they would like to change? As each situation is mentioned, ask one of the children to turn one of the arrows to face the other direction, and at the same time the camera should flash. Link this to Saul's experience by saying together, 'Shine your light, Lord, and help us to see things differently.'

— Theme 3 —

Famine and feast

Season: New Year

General introduction to the theme

The rhythm of famine and feast was part and parcel of life in the lands of the Bible. A lack of rainfall meant that there were often times when rivers dried up and the crops failed. Perhaps the most famous famine is the one that occurred when Joseph was governor in Egypt (Genesis 41:56–57), which brought his family from Canaan seeking help from Pharaoh's storehouses. The story of Ruth begins with a famine and these natural disasters are also recorded during the reign of King David (2 Samuel 21:1).

However, the idea of famine is also used in another sense in the big story of the Bible—a famine of hearing God's word (see Amos 8:11). Jesus picks up this idea when he quotes from Deuteronomy to silence the voice of his first temptation in the wilderness. He declares that human beings need more than food to be truly alive; they need all the words that come from God (Matthew 4:4; Deuteronomy 8:3). This sort of famine can cause a starvation of our souls, just as a physical famine does to our bodies. However, in the same way that the famine drove the sons of Jacob to travel to Egypt, opening up the path to reconciliation with their brother, so a famine of God's love can draw people back to God in repentance, as in the parable of the prodigal son (Luke 15:11–32).

In contrast to famine, it is noticeable how often Jesus uses the image of feasting in his stories, to describe the joy of being 'back home' with God. A party—and especially a wedding feast with plenty to eat—is frequently used to describe what heaven will be like (Matthew 8:11). The Jewish religious year is punctuated with festivals and feasting that, in different ways, point forward to the great celebration in heaven itself.

In this series we explore six 'famine and feast' stories from across the Bible that unpack this theme: the famines teach God's people that it is God alone who provides, and the feasts celebrate the joy of being friends again with God.

Reflective overview

A Bible, a bright plain circular tablecloth, sand to sprinkle, two serviettes, some matzo wafer and some wooden bird shapes, a piece of blue ribbon, a basket of wooden or toy fruits, dried grasses, a small roll of bread and a small jug, confetti, a plate, a wine cup, wine or juice that looks like wine, some smiling faces, five small wooden or toy rolls of bread and two fish, a paten and chalice (plate and Communion cup), a large bread roll, party poppers and streamers

Bible story: Matthew 4:4; John 6:60; Psalm 119:102–104

Action: *Open up the Bible and lay it down at your side.*

Script: God has given us the stories in his book to show us what he is like and how much he loves us. But what sort of stories are they?

Action: *Spread out a bright plain circular tablecloth. As you tell each part of the story, you will be laying out a place setting around the edge of the cloth. There are five around the edge and one in the centre. Start on the left, on the part of the circle nearest to you, and work round the cloth so that the stories appear clockwise for those listening on the other side.*

Script: They are like our daily bread. They are like a feast on a table. Some parts are hard to digest. Some parts are as sweet as honey. But we need every part.

Bible story: Exodus 16

Action: *Sprinkle some sand around the first place setting. On it, place an open serviette. On the serviette, place some pieces of wafer and some wooden bird shapes.*

Script: Long ago, God led his people out of Egypt. He led them on a long journey across the desert. The desert is an empty place and it's hard to find enough to eat. But every day God sent his people a sort of bread to eat called manna, and a sort of bird called quails. Day by day God fed his people in the desert.

Bible story: Numbers 13

Action: *Lay a piece of blue ribbon between the previous place setting and the next one. Set down an overflowing fruit basket on the other side of the ribbon, in the next place setting.*

Script: God wanted his people to live in a land of plenty. When they arrived at the River Jordan, Moses sent Joshua and some other spies into the land to see what it was like. The spies came back with pomegranates, figs and a bunch of grapes so big it took two men to carry it on a pole! There was plenty to eat in the land.

Bible story: 1 Kings 17

Action: *Place some dried-out grasses between the second and third place settings. Place a roll of bread and a small jug of oil on a plate in the third setting.*

Script: Even in the land of plenty, there were times of famine when there was no rain, so there wasn't enough to eat. During one famine, the prophet Elijah met a woman who was collecting sticks. She told him she was going to make a fire and use the last of her oil and flour to bake a little loaf of bread for herself and her son, and then they would die, as there was no food left. Elijah asked her to use the last of her flour to make a little loaf for him as well. He promised her that God wouldn't let the flour or the oil run out until it rained again. The woman kindly baked him some bread from the last of her flour and God kept the promise Elijah had made: she never ran out of flour or oil.

Bible story: John 2:1–10

Action: *For the next place setting, scatter some confetti between a plate and an empty wine cup. Pour wine into the cup.*

Script: Many years later, Jesus was at a wedding when his mother told him the wine had run out. The feast would be ruined. But Jesus changed some huge jars of water into wine and the feast could carry on even better than before.

Bible story: Luke 5:30–33; Luke 15:2; John 6:1–13, 22–35

Action: *Place smiling faces between the cup and a serviette. Spread out the serviette like a picnic rug. On the serviette, place five rolls and two fish shapes. Tear some bread and scatter it in a trail that links the serviette and the last plate and cup.*

Script: Jesus enjoyed many meals with his friends. In fact, he enjoyed so many meals that some people told him off for eating with the wrong people. One time, Jesus was out in the desert with thousands of people who were very hungry. One boy gave his food to Jesus and Jesus turned the five rolls and two fish into enough food for all the thousands of people. Jesus told everyone, 'I am the bread that gives life! No one who comes to me will ever be hungry.'

Bible story: Matthew 26:26–28

Action: *Place a plate and wine glass in the centre of the cloth. Tear a bread roll in two and place it on the plate as you speak. Pour out wine into the cup as you speak.*

Script: The last meal Jesus ate with his friends before he died was a feast to remember the time when God led his people out of Egypt. Jesus took the bread and said, 'Take this and eat it. This is my body, given for you.' He took the wine and said, 'Take this and drink it. This is my blood poured out for you.'

Bible story: Matthew 8:11

Action: *Spread some party streamers or party poppers over the table, around and between the plates. Sit back and spread out your hands over the table in enjoyment.*

Script: Jesus tells us that the kingdom of heaven is like a wonderful feast, with food for everyone to share—a feast that goes on and on and on!

Script: I wonder where we see the feast happening today…

I wonder why there is famine as well as feast in this story…

I wonder why Jesus said once that people don't just need food to eat but every word that comes from God…

Reproduced with permission from *The Big Story* published by BRF 2011 (978 1 84101 812 6) www.barnabasinchurches.org.uk 47

Feast in the desert
The story of manna and quails

Bible link

Exodus 16

You will need:

A map of Moses' journeys, some cooked cold chicken nuggets wrapped in foil, some pieces of rice paper or rice cake (also wrapped up, for hygiene purposes). If you can bear to, it would be really good to have some maggots (from an angling shop) in a piece of foil—but kept separate from the edible food. You will also need some craft equipment for 'Playing with the story'.

— The Barnabas Children's Bible —

Story 52

Background to the story

Moses led God's people out of slavery in Egypt to freedom. Then they were on their way to Mount Sinai and from there to the promised land of Canaan. However, quite soon after the excitement of crossing the Sea of Reeds, they found themselves struggling with their desert journey. The people began to complain and to wonder whether it might not have been better to stay in Egypt, where they were at least sure of where their next meal was coming from.

Open the story

On a biblical map showing the Sinai Desert, point out how far Moses and the people had come from Egypt. Ask the children to imagine that they have been travelling for a month and a half and there is nothing around them but desert. Sitting down, ask the children to imagine they are the Israelites. Ask them to look around. What can they see? Sparse, dry grass… rocks, caves, scorpions, snakes, sand…? What can they hear? What temperature is it? How does the desert make them feel? Encourage the children to conjure up a barren, bleak, exposed place.

Tell the story

Building on the imaginative opening above, ask the children to imagine the good food that would have been available in Egypt. Great pots of stew! Fruit! Watermelons! Bread! Garlic! Invite them to rub their tummies in memory of all those good meals. But here in the wilderness, there is… nothing. Everyone is very hungry. And when we get hungry, we get cross. God's people got cross with Moses. Invite the children to shake their fists, grumble and tell Moses what they think of him.

Choose a volunteer to be Moses. Sit that person in front of the others and let them grumble at him or her. Explain that God said to Moses, 'I will give you bread in the morning and meat in the evening. Then you will know I am the Lord your God.' Scatter some cold wrapped chicken nuggets around. That evening, lots of little birds called quails landed everywhere in the camp, so the people had meat to eat. Scatter some wrapped pieces of rice paper or rice cake around. When the people got up the next day and looked outside their tents, there on the ground was some strange, white, wafer-like stuff. They didn't know what it was, so they called it 'manna', which means 'what is this?' in Hebrew. Moses told them to collect enough for one day, but some people grabbed lots of it, more than they could eat. By the next day it was smelly and full of maggots.

Bring out the maggots (sensitively!) and explain that every day the same thing happened. In the morning the manna came down and in the evening the quails arrived. Every day, the people collected enough food for each day. However, on the day before the sabbath, they could collect two days' worth so that they didn't have to work on the sabbath. Each day they trusted that God would give them more on the next day—and, for 40 years, God did!

Talk about the story

Lay out a basic set for the story with a desert box or sand tray, some small card cones for tents, some small plastic or wooden figures for the people, some torn paper for manna and some bird shapes for quail. Ask the children to retell the story, moving around the set of objects. If they are not very forthcoming, try telling it yourself, with lots of mistakes for them to correct. Younger children might want to continue playing with the objects. As you look at the story set, ask, 'Why might God have given the people fresh food every day and not let them store it up for the next day? What things does God give us every day that can't be stored until the next day?'

Many years later, Jesus taught his friends a prayer. Perhaps he had this story in mind when he taught them one particular line. Ask the children which line of the Lord's Prayer they think goes best with the story.

Play with the story

Decorate the border of a sheet of A4 paper. Write the words 'Give us today our daily bread' in the middle. Invite the children to take the sheets home and fill them in, as a family, with the good things God gives them every day.

Alternatively, the children could decorate boxes or baskets and make little torn sheets of paper (manna) to put inside. On each piece of paper, invite them to write down a good thing God gives them during the week.

Reflect on the story

Hand out pieces of the rice paper or a rice cake to everyone and then ask the children to share ideas of what God gives us every day. Each time a suggestion is made, they should break off a piece and eat it in a short period of silence. End by saying the words of the Lord's Prayer together. If the prayer is unfamiliar to the children or there are younger children in the group, say one line at a time and ask them to repeat it. Repeat the lines of the prayer in the light of the story of the manna and the quails.

Although the manna only lasted one day, the Israelites never forgot how God looked after them every day. Ask the children to keep an eye open in the week ahead for the good things God provides for us.

Feast in the promised land

The story of the twelve spies sent to Canaan

Bible links

Numbers 13—14

You will need:

A Bible timeline, items for the observation game, a bunch of grapes divided into smaller bunches, a large piece of paper, glue, scissors, magazines or coloured pens, a downloaded activity or pictures from magazines from a charity or organisation that works to get food to people who have none

— The Barnabas Children's Bible —

Story 64

Background to the story

Under Moses' leadership, God's people reached the very borders of Canaan. God instructed Moses to choose twelve leaders to go ahead and explore the country, but the reports they brought back were mixed. Only Caleb and Joshua displayed the faith that was needed to take the land. The story of the twelve spies is a great one to explore because of its strong themes of trust and fear, provision and plenty.

Open the story

Use the timeline to show the children where the story comes in the Bible, or ask what they can tell you already about Moses. Find out if they know anything about Moses' young friend, Joshua. If they mention the walls of Jericho, explain that this story comes before that—before the people even got as far as Jericho.

Explore ideas of spying out the land with a simple game. Arrange for a table to be laid and covered with a range of interesting foods and other items. Include some mysterious objects and also some less attractive items of food. If possible, hide the table behind a screen or in a nearby room. Invite the children, one at a time, to go and view what is out of sight to the rest. Give them only a short time to do this and then ask them to report on what they saw. Comment on the similarities and differences in their descriptions. Who noticed the good things and who noticed the bad things? Explain that today's story is about twelve spies who had to report back to Moses and the others what they found in the promised land. It seems that they focused on different things!

Tell the story

Ask the children to act out the story below as you tell it. You'll need someone to play the roles of Moses, Joshua and Caleb. You could have someone to play God, any number of explorers and God's people who listen to what they saw. Smaller groups will need to double up on parts.

At the points marked with an ellipsis (…), stop and use drama ideas to explore the feelings of the characters at that moment before continuing with the story. For example, you could hot-seat the characters and ask them:

- How were you feeling when this happened?
- Why did you feel like that?
- What are you feeling about Moses at the moment?
- What are you feeling about God at the moment?

God rubbed his hands in excitement. He jumped up and down with glee. After walking through the wilderness for 40 years, at last his people had arrived at the edge of the promised land. The land he had been getting ready for them for years! The land that was full of good things to eat and drink! The land that had so much, it was as if it was flowing with milk and honey! God sat down and called to his friend Moses.

Moses took his sandals off, stood up and listened hard to get the instructions right. God told Moses to choose twelve leaders to send into the promised land to explore it. Moses nodded. He chose twelve leaders from the tribes of Israel and sat them down in front of him. He explained that he wanted them to go and see what the country was like, what the cities were like, and what the people were like. He asked them to bring back some fruit so that he could see how well it grew there…

The twelve explorers lined up and marched off across the River Jordan into the promised land. When they saw the countryside, their mouths fell open, and Joshua and Caleb did a high five. When they saw the cities, they trembled—except Joshua and Caleb, who were choosing where they would like to build their houses. And when they saw the giant people, their knees knocked together—except Joshua's and Caleb's. They were too busy thanking God for this lovely place where they were going to live…

The leaders cut down a bunch of grapes, so big that it took two men to carry it on a pole. Joshua and Caleb were the only ones whose eyes weren't goggling and whose knees weren't knocking, so they got to carry the grapes. They marched back to Moses and the people. The explorers sat down in front of the people, biting their nails. God rubbed his hands, ready to hear the explorers tell the people what a wonderful country they were going to live in. They said that the fruit was really good and God nodded happily.

Then they all said 'But!'—and it all came rushing out: the cities were huge and strong! And the people were enormous! The spies looked like grasshoppers next to them! The people would never win any wars against them! And all the people agreed, that sounded really scary. They didn't want to live there! …

God was really annoyed. He folded his arms. He'd gone to so much trouble to get a fantastic country ready for his people, and here they were, worrying their socks off. He didn't want his people to be scared; he wanted them to be happy. He gave Joshua and Caleb a prod. Joshua and Caleb spoke

up and told the people to trust God. They said they had to have that amazing land. It wouldn't be a problem. It didn't matter how big the people were, if God was on their side.

As it turned out, Joshua and Caleb were right. God's people had nothing to worry about. It didn't matter how big the people there were, or how strong the cities were. With God on their side, they could go in and enjoy the wonderful place that God had got ready for them. I expect they all enjoyed eating the grapes, too!

Talk about the story

The story throws up feelings of nervousness, trust, mistrust, adventure, excitement, fear, disappointment, puzzlement, faith and praise. Ask questions that relate those feelings to times when the children have felt the same. For example, talk about how nervous the explorers were about going into the promised land and invite the children to share times when they have been nervous about going somewhere new. How did they feel about God at that time?

Talk about the way that the promised land was full of wonderful things to eat and how much God wanted his people to be in a place full of good things to enjoy. Sometimes we call such a place a 'land of milk and honey'. What good things has God given us to enjoy?

Play with the story

Fill a big sheet of paper with pictures or cut-outs from magazines showing all the good things we enjoy: food, drink, toys, friends, beautiful places and so on. Try to make it as locally relevant as possible, including pictures of your local parks, hills, cafés, toy shops and so on.

We are so rich! Yet some parts of our country and our world are poor and don't enjoy all the good things God wants them to have. From a website or magazine, show an example of a country where people don't have enough to live on. Ask where else the children know of, that is not 'a land of milk and honey'.

Fill a second big sheet of paper with pictures you have downloaded from an aid organisation's website or obtained from their magazine.

As you work, talk about what the children could do to raise some money for organisations who try to redress the balance, such as Christian Aid, Tearfund or Oxfam. Perhaps the children could give up a luxury just for a week and give the money saved to an aid organisation?

Alternatively, suggest that they buy some fairly traded chocolate so that people who grow the beans and pick them are guaranteed a fair wage. Ask them to bring in the wrapper to glue on to the collage of good things.

Reflect on the story

Give small bunches of grapes to half the children, with strict instructions not to eat them yet. Point out that this half of the group has plenty of grapes, while the other half has none. In our world, many people have plenty of good things and many have none. Invite the children to share their grapes with those who have none, as a sign that they want to make the whole world a fairer place. As the children share the grapes, have a moment of quiet to ask God to help make the world a place where everyone has enough to eat.

NB: It might be worth having a few bunches of grapes in reserve in case of early consumption disasters. Alternatively, you might be able to make a memorable point out of the injustice when some people are greedy while others go without!

Feast in a drought
The story of Elijah and the widow's oil

You will need:

Ingredients and equipment for making unleavened (flat) bread (see below), hospitality resources (see below)

Matzah (unleavened bread)

225g plain flour (half white, half wholemeal)
Pinch of salt
1 tablespoon vegetable oil
Enough water to make a stiff dough

Knead the ingredients well together, roll into a thin rectangle, cut into squares, place on a greased baking tray and prick with a fork. Cook at 180°C/Gas Mark 5 for about 20 minutes, until golden brown.

— The Barnabas Children's Bible —

Story 163

Background to the story

When Israel was ruled by King Ahab, who, under the influence of his wife Jezebel, had introduced the worship of idols into the country, God sent Elijah to challenge the king to change his ways and to warn him that there would be no more rain until he did. The result was a severe famine in the land. Elijah was forced to run and hide from the authorities and found himself eventually at Zarephath in Sidon, on the coast to the north of Israel (in modern-day Lebanon). He found a welcome and food at the home of a widow and her young son.

We don't often expect children to exercise the gift of hospitality, but most children love acting as hosts, either in play or real life. This wonderful story is an inspiration to open up our homes and share whatever we have with each other, so that God can work miracles.

Open the story

Ask the children if they have ever been round to someone's home for a meal or if they have ever had somebody round for tea. Another word for this is 'hospitality', which is nothing to do with hospitals but is about being a 'host' to someone—welcoming a friend or guest into your home. God loves it when people are hospitable. He can do some of his most wonderful miracles when people are hospitable to each other. Children don't own their own homes yet, but with help and encouragement they can enjoy being hospitable to people, so that they can experience being part of God's miracles.

Tell the story

Make some unleavened bread together. As the children knead the dough, tell them the story of Elijah and the widow of Zarephath from 1 Kings 17:8–16. You could use the version in *The Barnabas Children's Bible*. Make the dough into shapes of loaves, or of a jar, Elijah, a widow or a young boy. Bake the dough and, while it is baking, ask some open-ended questions such as those below.

- I wonder how the widow felt when Elijah asked her for food…
- I wonder why she was prepared to share her last bit of food with him…
- I wonder how her son felt when he saw his mother take some food to Elijah…
- I wonder what you would say if someone asked you to share your last food with them…
- I wonder why God sent Elijah to the widow and didn't just give him some food…
- I wonder what is your favourite part of the story…

Talk about the story

Talk about the things that make people feel most welcome when they are invited to enjoy someone else's hospitality: a smile, a comfortable chair, good conversation, food and drink, a game…? Ask what other Bible stories or other stories the children can think of in which someone invites someone else to join them for food. Examples include Abram, Sarai and the three strangers (Genesis 18:1–15); Boaz and Ruth (Ruth 2:14); Jesus, Mary and Martha (Luke 10:38–42); Jesus and Zacchaeus (Luke 19:1–10); Paul and Lydia (Acts 16:11–15).

If the children are old enough to enjoy some independent research, ask them to discover what good things God made happen in the above examples of hospitality.

Play with the story

If possible, find a way of showing hospitality to other people. For example, you could serve refreshments to the rest of the church or to parents and carers as they collect the children. (They might need some warning to allow extra time.) Alternatively, you could bake or buy a cake together and invite another group round to eat it, such as older members of your church, younger children or the youth group. Again, you could organise a party, or serve coffee after the church service, or perhaps you could organise a safari meal with each course being eaten in a different house. When you have decided what to do, plan to deliver this hospitality to others, practising making people welcome and putting them at ease.

Reflect on the story

Eat the bread figures, saying a prayer before you eat them to ask God to help you all enjoy the miracles he brings out of being hospitable to other people.

The feast at the wedding
The story of the miracle at Cana

Bible link

John 2:1–12

You will need:

A picture of the wedding at Cana downloaded from the internet, cardboard, glasses, pots, water, wine, craft materials, digital camera (optional)

— The Barnabas Children's Bible —

Story 258

Background to the story

This miracle is recorded in John 2:1–12 as the first of Jesus' special signs. As such, it is both the story of what happened at a wedding that Jesus attended, not far from his home town of Nazareth, and the account of something important about who Jesus really is. Mary and Jesus' first disciples were also at the wedding, so it may well have been the marriage celebration of a relative. The host would have been severely embarrassed by any shortage of wine, particularly as the occasion would have lasted several days in the Jewish culture of the day. Jesus not only secretly rescued the party but he also taught his friends (and, interestingly, the servants) that he had come to bring in a new and extravagant experience of God's love. Six water jars full of vintage wine would be a huge amount.

Open the story

Very briefly, talk about the start of Jesus' ministry: his baptism, his temptations and how he started preaching and healing. Say that today's story is about the very first of Jesus' miracles. Does anyone know what it might be? Using pieces of cardboard, slowly uncover a picture of the wedding at Cana or simply of wine. Reveal the picture a little at a time so that the children can guess what the picture is.

As a way into the story, play a game in which each person has to collect water via a straw and deposit it in a 500ml plastic bottle or carton at the far end of the room. Place the bottle in some other container, such as a washing-up bowl, to guard against spillage. At the opposite end, have a supply of water in a large jug. Give everyone a straw. Each person in turn should suck up some water into the straw, put their finger over the end, carry the water carefully in this way and then deposit it in the plastic bottle. How long does it take to fill the bottle? In the story, there were six jars, each of which held between 20 and 30 gallons of water. That is the equivalent of over 1000 bottles full of water that became wine.

Tell the story

Tell the story, using the children as actors and using wine glasses (preferably plastic for safety), a table and six large pots, washing-up bowls, big saucepans or similar items as props. You might want to take photos for your drama, if you have permission from parents and prime carers.

There are plenty of parts to play: the groom and the bride, the man in charge of the drinks (the steward), the guests, the servants, Jesus, the disciples, Mary, and the messenger who must have told Mary that the wine was running out. Prepare some small prompt cards for each of the different actors involved, with some key sentences to say. Now give the children time to put the whole drama together, encouraging them to imagine themselves into the parts and to use some additional appropriate dialogue. Suggestions for the prompt cards might include:

- Groom: This is my wedding day. I want everyone to have a good time.
- Bride: This is the happiest day of my life.
- Messenger who came to Mary: Excuse me, Mary, but we're down to our very last bottle of wine.
- Mary: I'll talk to Jesus. (To Jesus) My son, they need your help. They've run out of wine and the party will be ruined. (To the servants) Do whatever he tells you.

- Disciples: What is Mary saying to Jesus? I wonder what Jesus is up to.
- Jesus: It's not really the right time and place for miracles. I don't think I should get involved.
- The servants: What a strange thing to be asked to do! We'd better take a glass to the steward.
- Steward: Wow, this wine is really good. Why leave the best to last?
- Guests: This is a great party! I wonder what the servants and Jesus were up to. Wow, the wine tastes better now than it did at the beginning.

Talk about the story

In turn, hot-seat Mary, a wedding guest, the bride and a disciple to find out what they thought of the miracle. Try to establish how disastrous it would have been if there had been no wine for the party. Discuss together what the story tells us about who Jesus is.

What might have been the reasons why Jesus kept his actions secret from the host and guests at the wedding? How might we respond to those who believe that this story could lead some people to think that Jesus had just come to do party tricks or, worse, even to encourage people to drink too much? The story of the wedding at Cana is quoted at the beginning of every marriage service that uses words from the Church of England prayer book. Why might this be and what might it mean to a bride and groom today?

Play with the story

Make a big poster display for the story together. Choose a masterpiece painting of the marriage at Cana. Divide it into squares and ask each child to copy and enlarge a version of that square on to a piece of card or paper, and then reassemble them all on your display as your own version of the picture. Also, you could include digital photos of the scenes the children acted out earlier. Alternatively, using two large card wine glass shapes, glue on mosaic paper pieces of blue (for the water glass) and red (for the wine glass).

Reflect on the story

Create a focal point of a glass of water and a glass of wine. Explain that Jesus loves to change disasters into miracles, to change really bad times into really good times.

Prepare two small cups for each person. In one cup have a small amount of water, and in the other a small amount of a red liquid (possibly red grape juice, cranberry juice or cherryade). Encourage the children to mention different things that they want to ask God to change for the better. As each person says something, pause for a moment and invite everyone to pick up and sip some of the water and then some of the other drink. Encourage them to go on praying for people or places that are going through a bad time, asking Jesus to turn those situations into great times instead.

The feast at the picnic
The story of feeding the 5000

Bible links

Matthew 14:13–21; Mark 6:30–44; Luke 9:10–17;
John 6:1–14

You will need:

A plate, some pictures or symbols for the loaves and
fish

— The Barnabas Children's Bible —

Story 275

Background to the story

The story of the feeding of the 5000 is recorded in all
four Gospels and is probably one of the most well-
known and well-loved of Jesus' miracles. Each writer
highlights a different aspect of the story's importance.
It shows the compassion Jesus had for the crowds,
who were 'like sheep without a shepherd' (Mark 6:34);
it demonstrates the overwhelming provision of God,
who supplies more than enough for our need; it points
forward mysteriously to the breaking and sharing of
bread that happened at the last supper; it introduces
the gift of the child, which makes it all possible; it gives
a special significance to the numbers involved, which
invites speculation; and it has something deep to teach
about faith—something even Jesus' close disciples
missed, which led him to remonstrate with them later,
saying, 'Don't you understand? Have you forgotten
about the five thousand people and all those baskets
of leftovers from just five loaves of bread?' (Matthew
16:9).

Open the story

Give a blockbuster-type build-up to the importance of
the story. See if the children can guess what's coming.

* It's a massive story with a cast of thousands.
* It's a big story involving all age groups.
* It's an important story that is told four times in the
  Bible.
* It's a special story that could have happened only
  because one child said 'yes' to Jesus.
* If you have done some of the following things, then
  this story is for you: been on a long walk; been in a
  rowing boat; eaten too much; listened to someone
  telling stories; felt very hungry; picked up litter; had
  a big surprise; eaten freshly caught fish; made some
  bread; given away something very precious; found it
  hard to do the right thing.
* And finally, this story has some very strange number
  work: something was added together, then divided,
  and then multiplied, so that more was taken away at
  the end than was there at the beginning!
* Can you guess what story is coming?

Tell the story

Divide the children into four groups, even if there is
only one person for each part. Invite each group or
person in turn to act out the story in mime as you tell it.

1. Jesus and his friends had been working hard, telling
   the good news about God's love. It was time for a
   rest. They rowed over to a lonely place. Jesus was
   also sad because his friend John had been killed.
   They found a quiet place to be.

2. The people of the towns loved Jesus' stories. They
   wanted to hear more. You may remember some of
   the stories he told. (Suggest some but get the titles
   slightly wrong, inviting the children to correct
   you—for example, the lost goat, the runaway
   daughter, the story of the farmer who knew how
   to sew, the story of the man who found a precious
   diamond, the story of building a house on tarmac,

the story of throwing a big birthday party, the story of the hungry caterpillar, the story of the ten talons, and so on.) So the crowd got up and ran all around the shore, looking for Jesus. Suddenly they found him in the quiet lonely place.

3. Jesus saw them coming. The disciples' reaction was, 'Oh no!' but Jesus reassured them that the people needed to hear more stories about God's love. So Jesus started to tell more stories. The people got so lost in the stories that it went past lunch time and they were getting hungry. Jesus asked Philip to feed them all. How many hamburgers? How many packets of chips? How many chicken pieces? How much will it cost? Then Andrew brought a child who had a packed lunch—just five rolls and two fish. The disciples laughed, but Jesus knew that it was enough.

4. Jesus took the bread and the fish and he broke them into pieces. Then Jesus said 'thank you' to God and gave the pieces to his friends to hand out to the crowds. More and more food kept appearing as the disciples kept handing out the pieces. More and more and more kept appearing; everyone was amazed.

Talk about the story

Explain that you want to find out the difference between being a real disciple of Jesus and just someone who comes and listens to him for a day. Ask the children each to choose to be one of the people from the story. Ask them to think of that person's name and what they might do as a job or during the rest of their time. (Make sure you have some who are disciples and some who are members of the crowd.) Now hot-seat the people from the crowd and the disciples. If necessary, give out some questions beforehand. (The children may not need this stimulus, preferring to think of their own questions to ask.)

- What's your name?
- How old are you?
- What do you normally do?
- Why have you come to hear Jesus?
- What do you think of him?
- Why do you like Jesus / not like Jesus?
- What has he done today?
- Will you come and see him tomorrow?
- What would you do if Jesus asked you to do something difficult for him?

- How would you feel if Jesus asked you to give up everything and follow him?
- Do you think you would follow Jesus if you knew he was going to be killed in a few years' time?
- Would you like to get to know Jesus better? Why / why not?
- If you had the choice, how much time would you spend listening to Jesus?
- What do you think of the idea of hanging out with the rest of Jesus' disciples?

You could finish by asking, 'If you were in Jerusalem a little while later and saw Jesus on his way to the cross, do you think you would care or not?'

Play with the story

There are many possible meanings to this story, and each person may be thinking of something different that is important to them. It would therefore be appropriate to let everyone choose what they want to make in response to what they have heard, rather than prescribing what they should produce. To do this, have a collection of craft materials available, such as paper in various colours, crayons and colouring pens, paints, items for a collage, clay, scissors, glue sticks and so on. Invite the children to decide what they would like to do next as a way of exploring what the story has meant for them.

Reflect on the story

One way to apply the story to our lives is to think about the decision taken by the young child to give his packed lunch to Jesus. Sit the children in a circle and place an empty plate in the centre. Cut up pictures or use symbols of the five loaves and two small fish, placing them together to one side. Explain that the child had no idea what was going to happen. He didn't know that he would get some food back if he handed over his meal. It was a big ask!

Invite the children to pray about any big decisions of trust that they or others they know may have to make in the days ahead. After they have talked about this, or after a silence, ask them one at a time to take one of the food pictures or symbols from the pile and put it on the plate as an act of prayerful trust in Jesus for that situation. You might like then to add lots more bread and fish symbols on top as a sign that God promises to provide all that we need and much more.

The feast of feasts

The story of the last supper

Bible links

Matthew 26:26–30; Mark 14:22–26; Luke 22:14–23

You will need:

Items for the sounds of Holy Week (see below), a cloth and various items of food (depending on how much of a Passover meal you plan to set out), a cut-out or black-and-white picture of bread and wine, crayons

— The Barnabas Children's Bible —

Story 303

Background to the story

It is the evening before the day when Jesus is to be tried, condemned and crucified. We are in the back streets of Jerusalem in an upstairs room. Jesus is celebrating a traditional Passover meal but he adds some strange new words and actions to the usual liturgy, that puzzle his friends. He is trying to prepare them for what is about to happen and also pointing forward to what his death will mean, not just for them but for the whole world.

This session comprises a re-enactment of the last supper from Matthew's account, with a little bit from Luke. It concentrates on the bread and wine rather than the foot-washing. If you have a particular sacramental tradition in your church, you might want to check with your leader that she or he is happy with what you plan to do. If they are not happy, perhaps they would be able to lead the session for you or provide you with material that they consider suitable.

Open the story

Put the importance of the story into its proper context by building up to it with some of the sounds of Holy Week. You will need to collect a series of items to make sound effects, such as two halves of a coconut for a donkey's hooves; a tray of gravel, deep enough to allow a child to stand in and march vigorously on the spot; a collection of pieces of wood that can be thrown down noisily; a bag of coins that can be jangled and from which some can be tipped out; a wooden platter and spoon; a cup and some liquid to pour into it; some pieces of matzo bread or cracker that will snap noisily; a bowl of water. As you introduce the sound effects, invite some of the children to come up and take responsibility for making a particular sound. In addition to all the objects listed above, some other sound effects are made with hands and voices. These sounds include cheering, whispering, pigeon and sheep noises, and gasps of breath.

Explain that, between them, the children are going to provide the soundtrack for the most important week of Jesus' life, leading up to today's story. These sounds will help them enter into the events of what Christians call Holy Week.

The sounds represent:

- Palm Sunday on the streets: the clip-clop of donkey's hooves; the cheering of the crowds; some suspicious whispering behind hands; the overturning of the tables in the temple; the sounds of pigeons cooing, sheep bleating and coins being rattled; the sound of pieces of wood dropping to the ground and then some coins falling; the gasps of breath from the onlookers.
- The Roman soldiers marching and discussions with Judas about betrayal: the crunch of marching feet made by soldiers on the move; the sound of people telling others to keep quiet; the sound of a money bag being placed into someone else's hands.
- The events of the last supper: the sounds of washing; the noise of a spoon scraping a wooden platter during a meal; the sound of drink being pouring into a cup; the sound of matzo being cracked; the sound of puzzled questioning; the sound of a door slamming shut.

Tell the story

Try to recreate the atmosphere at the last supper and help the children to enter into the intimacy, the mystery, the 'family-traditional-celebration-meal-they-had-done-since-they-were-little' feel to the supper, and then the renewing and reinvigorating of the old tradition as Jesus turns it on its head.

Ask the children to imagine that they are Jesus' disciples. They have been with him for three years. What have they seen in those three years? What stories have they heard him tell? What miracles has Jesus done? What sort of a person have they discovered him to be? What do they like best about him?

Imagine that you are in Jerusalem, the capital city. Recall the events of the previous Sunday: the crowds cheering Jesus on as he came riding in on a donkey... and then Jesus clearing all those nasty money changers out of the temple. Imagine you have been watching Jesus all week, with the Pharisees getting crosser and crosser at the things he's said about God and about them. Imagine you have been out in public with Jesus and with him in the crowds all week. But tonight is different. Tonight it's just Jesus and you—his disciples. Imagine the cosiness of the room with all the doors shut and the curtains closed.

It's a very special festival tonight, the festival of the Passover. As one of Jesus' disciples, you would always have had a special meal to celebrate this festival, ever since you were little. Now you are really pleased that you're going to be sharing it with Jesus this time. Imagine that you are getting everything ready for him.

(Set the table for a simple Passover meal, placing down some of the items from a traditional Seder plate. Alternatively, just lay a cloth with a cup of blackcurrant juice and a plate holding a bread roll or matzo, and just act out the bread and wine part of the story.)

Ask the children to imagine that they are sharing in the celebration family meal together—just as they would have done when they were little. During the meal, though, Jesus does something strange. He takes the bread and he breaks it. Then he says, 'Take this and eat it. This is my body. Eat this and remember me.'

(Pass round the bread. Pause to reflect on how the children might feel if they had been one of the disciples.)

Then Jesus takes the wine and says, 'This is my blood, and with it God makes his agreement with you. It will be poured out, so that many people will have their sins forgiven. From now on I am not going to drink any wine, until I drink new wine with you in my Father's kingdom.'

(Pass round the drink with a napkin to wipe the lip of the cup after each person sips. Pause to reflect on how the children might feel if they had been one of the disciples. What does Jesus mean? How do they feel? What do they think is going to happen next?)

Talk about the story

Talk about the bread and the wine. How does it feel that we have all eaten a piece of the same bread and sipped the same wine? What is special about bread? What is special about wine? How important do the bread and wine feel? What other stories are there in the Bible about bread or wine? Do these stories help us to understand what Jesus was doing in today's story? Can we ever understand completely everything there is to know about Jesus? Does it matter if we don't? Talk about what you do at the Eucharist or Communion in your church. What is the same as the last supper and what is different? Ask the children: if they were in charge of giving everyone in their church bread and wine to remember Jesus by, how would they do it?

Play with the story

Give out large cut-outs of bread on a plate and of a wine glass. Ask the children to explore the mystery of the last supper by creating their own drawings on the shapes.

Reflect on the story

Show the children a well-known work of art depicting the scene of the last supper. Ask them to think of one question they would want to ask Jesus if they were sitting at the table with him in the picture. Explain that the first disciples actually asked:

- Who is the greatest?
- Where are you going?
- How can we know the way there?
- How will you show yourself to us and not the world?
- Who will betray you?

In a moment of silence, invite the children to ask their questions of God and then to wait quietly for the answers that might come, then or later. It might help to play some reflective music at this point, such as the music to 'Broken for me, broken for you'.

— Theme 4 —

Death and life

Season: Lent to Easter

General introduction to the theme

When God made people, he breathed into them the breath of his life. There was no death in the beginning—creation bubbled and sparkled with life—but people chose to disobey God's life-giving instructions and death came into the world. Death brought an ending—it hurt and it destroyed—but God is a God of life, and again and again in the stories of the Bible we read how he brought life out of death for those who trusted in him. Finally, God sent Jesus to bring us life in all its fullness. He raised people to life from death and he gave them a new beginning. On the cross, Jesus chose death so that death itself could be turned upside down. Now, for all who follow Jesus, death is not the end.

Reflective overview

You will need:

A pale base cloth; a large circle of pale blue felt or net; a brown felt tree shape; green gauze or net cut into a leafy tree shape; seven teardrops made from blue or grey felt; a cross shape to fit over the tree trunk and branches (double-sided brown and green); seven small bright green felt leaf shapes; four larger leaves (double-sided, with an autumnal brown on one side and a fresh green on the other), decorated as follows on the green side:

- Leaf 1: a rainbow
- Leaf 2: a bronze snake
- Leaf 3: a human figure
- Leaf 4: a white human figure filled with teardrops, which folds back to reveal a human shape filled with a sunrise (try stitching a hinge on the figure's hand)

NB: This story takes the colours of green to represent life, mirroring spring-time leaves, and brown to represent death, like dead leaves in the autumn. The tree of life implicitly forms the structure of the story, with the cross superimposed on it.

Please be sensitive to the fact that your listeners may well have had experience of death and bereavement, and the story may provoke strong emotions. The repeated litany 'Death is an ending; death hurts; but God is a God of life' acknowledges the pain of bereavement but points towards a bigger picture.

Bible story: 1 Timothy 6:16

Action: *Place the open Bible to the side of the large pale base cloth.*

Script: God has given us stories in his book to show us what he is like.
God is a God of life.

Bible story: Genesis 2

Action: *Spread out a pale blue circle on top of the base cloth. Place the tree outline on top of the blue, and the green gauze haze over the tree.*

Script: When God made the first man, he breathed the breath of life into him and put him in the garden, where the tree of life grew. The man was surrounded by life. Life bubbled up through the earth in streams of water. Life was in every tree, fish, bird and animal. Life was in the woman God made. Their job was to take care of that place and to make more life. There was no death in that place.

Bible story: Genesis 3

Action: *Remove the green gauze so that the stark brown trunk is left. Scatter teardrops (rain-drops) behind the tree.*

Script: But when the man and the woman chose the wrong way, death came to them and to the world.

Bible story: Genesis 6—9

Action: *Place the four leaves, brown side up, at the ends of the branches.*

Script: Death is an ending; death hurts; but God is a God of life. God did not want his story to have this ending. He did not want his people hurt. He chose to bring life out of death.

Action: *Turn over one leaf to reveal the rainbow.*

Script: Death came to many people in the great flood. But God saved animals and people to fill the earth with life again. The rainbow was a sign that God promises life.

Bible story: Numbers 21:4–9

Action: *Turn over the leaf with the bronze snake behind it.*

Script: Death came to God's people in the desert and many died of snakebite. But God told Moses to set a bronze snake on a pole so that whoever looked at it would live. The bronze snake was a sign that God wants life.

Bible story: Ezekiel 37

Action: *Turn over the leaf with the person outline on it.*

Script: Ezekiel saw beyond the visible world into a valley of dry bones that first came together as skeletons, then grew flesh and muscles and skin, and then changed into people who came to life when a wind blew on them. The living people were a sign that God brings new life.

Bible story: Luke 7:11–17; John 11:25; John 10:10; John 11:35

Action: *Turn over the leaf with the teardrop figure.*

Script: Jesus said, 'I am the one who raises the dead to life… I came so that everyone would have life, and have it fully.' Jesus hated death. He was angry at the ending and the hurt that death brings. Once, full of compassion, he brought back to life the son of a poor widow, and later, when his friend Lazarus died, he wept.

Bible story: John 11:1–44

Action: *Fold out the teardrop figure to reveal the sunrise figure.*

Script: Jesus brought Lazarus back from death and made him alive again. Jesus brought new beginnings. Jesus brought healing. Jesus brought life in all its fullness.

Bible story: Revelation 21; Romans 5; John 10:10

Action: *Place a brown cross over the tree trunk and branches.*

Script: But so that we could have life, Jesus chose death. This is a mystery. Life was buried in death. Death is an ending; death hurts; but God is a God of life.

Action: *Turn over the cross to reveal its bright green side.*

Script: When Jesus died, death turned upside down. Jesus died but came back to life. Because of Jesus, death is not just an ending but a beginning.

Action: *Take away the teardrops from the background. Scatter bright green leaves all over the tree.*

Script: Because of Jesus every tear will be wiped from our eyes. Because of Jesus we see that our God is a God of life. Death came into the world through one man, but life came into the world through one man. This is a new life, a life without ending, a life in all its fullness.

Death is an ending; death hurts; but God is a God of life.

Second start

The story of Noah and the flood

Bible links

Genesis 8:1—9:17

You will need:

A piece of white cloth or a white sheet, liquid stain remover and warm water, olive-coloured leaves (hidden around the meeting space beforehand), the outline of a tree drawn on a sheet of paper, colouring pens, rainbow coloured wool or wool in different rainbow colours

— The Barnabas Children's Bible —

Stories 6, 7 and 8

Background to the story

Genesis 6—9 recounts the story of the great flood and how God rescued Noah and his family from death, along with a selection of all the creatures, in order to give them and the world a second start. The framework of the story is God's deep sorrow at the way in which death had entered into his world (Genesis 6:5–6) because of the wrong choices people made, and God's decision to start all over again (v. 17). The story ends with God's instructions to Noah to repopulate the earth and to care for it (Genesis 9:1–7), which is an echo of God's original instructions to Adam and Eve in Genesis 1:28. God wants life, not death, and one sign that life will not be destroyed again is the rainbow that appears in the sky at the end of the story (9:12–17). This story reminds us that God's promise of life is stronger than death and that God is a God of life.

Open the story

Set the scene by asking the children whether they have ever made anything by themselves that they have been proud of. Now ask if they've ever experienced seeing the thing they had made damaged and spoilt. How did they feel? Finally, ask if they have ever had the further experience of seeing the thing they had made being repaired and mended. You could play this as a game by asking the children to cross the circle in response to these questions and then stopping to hear some of their stories.

God also made something he was proud of, which he declared was really good. God's creation was the world and everything in it, including us, but God's world became broken. What had been full of life now contained what was destructive, along with hurt and pain. Death spoilt God's world, but God longed to repair it, to start again—to turn death back to life.

Tell the story

As a visual aid, use a large piece of clean white cloth (an old sheet would be fine). This represents the world as it was made at the beginning, full of brightness and life. Now smudge some soil or dirt on to the cloth to show how death spoiled what was good. God wanted to start again—to wash the sheet clean, as it were.

Next, put the cloth into some warm water that already has some liquid stain remover added. Show the children how the stain begins to disappear (at least, it does in the adverts!).

The flood story tells us that God doesn't want death, hurt and destruction in his world. He wants to get rid of those things. It also tells us that people who trust in God will be kept safe—in this case, within the ark.

NB: If the stain doesn't completely disappear, maybe this is more appropriate than it might seem. The stain of disobedience described in Genesis 3 was still in the world even after the flood.

Even when the rain stopped, the flood waters took a long time to go down. It was a very thorough wash! The story says that Noah sent out first a raven and then a dove (more than once) in order to discover whether there was life again on earth. God was looking for life. Life in the story is symbolised initially by a green leaf from an olive tree.

To enter into this part of the story, set the children off on a search of the meeting space for 'life' in the form of leaves (olive leaves, if possible, or at least olive-coloured), which you have hidden. Arrange the leaves they find on to the outline of a tree so that the tree slowly comes to life.

Talk about the story

While they were in the ark, waiting for life to start all over again, Noah's family would have had time to think about how spoilt the world had become and how much God longed for it to be full of life, not death. Ask the children the following questions:

- If you had the chance to start the world all over again, what are the most important things that would be needed?
- In what ways would this new world be different from today's world?
- How could you make sure that there was no hurt, pain, destruction and death to spoil this world again?
- Complete a sentence that starts: 'My ideal world will be one where…'

Link the answers to God's longing for life for us all.

Play with the story

The story ends with the sign of the rainbow. Match each of the colours of the spectrum to feelings, moods, objects, situations and people that are life-giving in some way. Divide the colours up among the children and ask them to draw their ideas of something that is full of life in that particular colour. For example, red smiling lips, a beautiful red rose, a flame on a birthday cake candle, an orange tangerine, a refreshing orange drink, a bright orange kite in the sky, a bright yellow sun, a gleaming gold ring, the glorious beach in summer and so on.

Reflect on the story

With the children sitting in a circle, use some rainbow-coloured wool or wools of different colours to create a web of connections between them. As each child receives and passes on the wool, stop to think about the ways in which life is stronger than death and God wants us to begin again—in our homes, at school, at church and in the world. Also celebrate and give thanks for some of the life-giving images that the children may have drawn in the exercise with the rainbow colours (see above).

Twists and turns
The story of Moses and the bronze serpent

Bible links

Numbers 21:4–9; John 3:14–16; 2 Kings 18:4

You will need:

Balls of coloured string or wool, paper plates, scissors, Plasticine, craft sticks, a bamboo pole

— The Barnabas Children's Bible —

Story 68

Background to the story

Again and again the people of God became rebellious as they followed Moses through the desert. Their arrival at the promised land was a long time coming, and life back in Egypt seemed more attractive—even a life of slavery. Again and again God provided for the people, but their memories were short, and the disaster in today's story wasn't the first to happen to them. There was a whole series of plagues, rebellions and murmurings as the people lost faith and turned away from God.

God used defeat in battle, hunger, natural disasters and illness to bring them back to faith again. In the story of Moses and the serpent, God provided an antidote to the poison of the plague of fiery snakes. The story is one to which Jesus himself related: the serpent on the pole became an Old Testament pointer to the cross (see John 3:14–16). However, the bronze serpent was destined to become a snare, and hundreds of years later King Hezekiah had to have it destroyed because the people had turned it into an idol to be worshipped (see 2 Kings 18:4). How easily we forget and abuse God's gift of life!

Open the story

To introduce the story, you will need some balls of string or wool to give out to each child. The journeys of the people of God through the desert were full of twists and turns. Invite each child in turn to plot a path from an object on one side of the room to an object on the other. As they do so, they should let out the string or wool to show the path they have taken. The idea is to have as many twists and turns as possible as they cross to the other side, but without crossing over their own path at any point. When everyone has done this, the floor should be a maze of twists and turns.

How long a simple journey can become! How frustrating such a journey must have been! This is how it felt for the people in today's story. The journey to the promised land was taking for ever and they were fed up. They were angry with God, with Moses and with the sheer repetition of day after day in the desert with the same food and the same company. But it was then that the twists and turns became a plague of snakes! Ask the children to imagine all their twists and turns now turning into a plague of poisonous snakes.

Tell the story

Life in the desert was never easy. There were many dangers, including desert snakes. The snakes were poisonous and their bite was deadly. People were killed and many suffered without hope of a cure. Ask the children to imagine what it must have been like in the camp when this happened. What would the people be feeling? What would they be saying? But people soon forgot to complain because they were so busy trying to avoid the snakes and bringing help to those who had been bitten.

Play a game in which each child in turn has to try to step across the meeting space to the other side without treading on any of the snakes (that is, the lines of wool or string that they laid down earlier). Can they tiptoe across, only stepping on the spaces in between?

The people also began to realise that the plague of snakes was God's way of bringing them to their senses. God had always helped them at every twist and turn in the past, so why had God let them down now? When faced by the disaster, the people began to pray. What sort of prayers might they have said? Ask the children for some suggestions. (Perhaps they would have included prayers of saying sorry, cries for help, and requests for healing and a cure.)

The people asked Moses to pray for them. God had spoken through Moses so many times on their journeys—for example, when faced by the seemingly uncrossable Sea of Reeds, at Mount Sinai, when they were hungry and thirsty, and when they were faced by enemy forces. What might Moses have said to God? Ask the children for suggestions about what Moses might have prayed.

God's instructions to Moses turned out to be very strange. The answer to their prayer was unexpected. Moses was to forge a model snake out of bronze and attach it to a pole.

To enact this, gather together all the ends of the string or wool at one end of the room, while the children pick up the ends of their pieces at the other. Ask the children to plait the pieces together into one big, thick, long 'snake'. Tape the plaited snake together at the bottom and top and then wrap it around a long bamboo pole. Place the pole in the middle of the meeting space and tell the children what happened next. Moses told the people to look at the bronze snake and live.

By lifting the snake up on the pole, the people would have understood that this was putting the snake to death. It was a way of saying, 'Look, it can't harm us any more, because it's dead'. As they believed this to be true—that God had killed off the threat of death among them and that they would be safe and well— that's what happened. By looking to the serpent on the pole, everyone was saying, 'I believe that God has taken the killing away.' They had come back to faith again and God had turned death into life.

Talk about the story

Just as the bronze snake on the pole represented the killing off of the danger from the snakes, so Jesus said that his coming death on the cross would kill off all the poison that destroys the good in us. Read John 3:14–16. Why might Jesus have used the story of Moses and the snake to give Nicodemus a clue to life and death, rather than the more familiar Passover story?

Christians believe that, by looking to Jesus, they can have a death-to-life experience whenever they feel the power of bad things dragging them down. In what ways might the story help us to understand Easter better?

Later, the serpent on the pole became an idol, which people worshipped (2 Kings 18:4). Is there a danger that the cross or crucifix can become misused in this way?

Play with the story

To connect up the two stories (Numbers 21:4–9 and John 3:14–16), show the children how to make a simple cross from two craft sticks. Next, on a paper plate, ask them to draw an unbroken line from the outside rim in a spiral that winds its way to the centre. Cut along this line to make a curly snake. Colour in the snake. Attach the paper plate snake to the top of the upright stick.

The incident with the poisonous snakes brought the people back to faith in God. Sometimes it is only when bad times hit us or we deliberately get into a mess that we realise just how much we have forgotten to trust God. To show this visually, hand out some pieces of Plasticine and help the children to spell the word 'snake' in Plasticine letters on a piece of card. Put the craft activity of the snake on the pole next to the letters and ask the children to reshape each letter to become the five letters of the word 'faith' instead.

Reflect on the story

Gather in a circle and place a cross in the middle. Give each child a piece of wool long enough to extend from where they are sitting to the cross. Ask each child to gently twist and turn the wool around the fingers of one hand. As they do so, connect this action to the way in which we often twist and turn away from God and get ourselves into a mess. Next, one at a time around the circle, invite each child to untwist the wool. Giving help where needed, attach one end of each piece of wool to the cross while the children hold on to the other. Each time this has been completed, say together, 'We look to Jesus, who turns death to life, so we can start again.' While everyone is holding on to their wool attached to the cross, share other prayers together.

Alive again

The story of Ezekiel and the valley of dry bones

Bible links

Ezekiel 37:1–14

You will need:

A skeleton model or card parts of a skeleton (search on the internet for templates), musical instruments, CD of quiet music, dry leaves, a wooden cross, drawing pins, green leaves

— The Barnabas Children's Bible —

Stories 222–225

Background to the story

Ezekiel was with the first group of Jews to be taken into exile at the beginning of the sixth century BC. What the prophet Jeremiah and others had warned about, but what seemed impossible to many people, had taken place: God's people had been defeated and apparently abandoned. No last-minute rescue or miraculous escape had happened this time. They were captive again—this time, not in Egypt but in Babylon.

It must have been hard to come to terms with their plight. Had God been too weak to defend them? Had God given up on them? Why had God hidden himself when they needed him most? All this must have been in Ezekiel's mind as he tried to make sense of it all, but God gave Ezekiel a series of visions that promised new life for the people. In the story, Ezekiel sees a valley of dry bones, which represent the exiled people of God. 'Can these bones come back to life?' asks God. Ezekiel is given words to speak over the bones and then the dead army dramatically comes back to life.

Open the story

To introduce the theme, put all the separate bones of the skeleton model on to a tray of sand or dried earth. Talk about what the bones might make if you put them together, and then make up the skeleton together. Ask the children how they know it's not alive. What would it need to live? Say that some people feel very dried up and dead, even when they are alive. Sometimes writers run out of ideas for poems; teachers lose the energy to teach; asylum seekers feel far away from anyone who loves them; friends find they no longer enjoy each other's company. Who else might feel like these dry, dusty bones? Have the children ever felt like this?

Tell the story

Explain that there was a time when God's people felt like dry, dusty old bones. They were far from home in a foreign land, brought there by their enemies, and they longed to go home. They had lost all hope, but God didn't want them to stay hopeless. He wanted them to believe his promise that one day he would fill them with the Holy Spirit and bring them home again. God showed one of his prophets, a priest called Ezekiel, an amazing picture. What might the vision have sounded like to Ezekiel?

Provide a selection of instruments and materials for making sound effects, especially anything that makes a rattling noise (claves, shakers, hollow wooden shapes), a blowing noise (woodwind instruments or rain sticks), a rustling noise (tissue paper or brown paper) and the noise of stamping feet (anything drum-like).

Act out the story, with some children playing the parts of the bones and others providing sound effects as the bones come to life.

Talk about the story

Invite someone to be Ezekiel and everyone else to be the people of Israel, who haven't yet heard about Ezekiel's vision. Hot-seat some of the people to find out how they are feeling. Next, hot-seat Ezekiel to ask him about what he's just seen. Then hot-seat more people to see whether Ezekiel's vision has made a difference to the way they feel about God. Lastly, put Ezekiel back in the hot seat and, as present-day people, ask him questions to help find out what his vision might mean to us today.

Ask the children if they can sum up what they have discovered about God from the story.

Play with the story

Make individual skeletons. Add basic body shapes, facial features, hands and feet. Design clothes with fold-over tabs and dress the figures in them.

Reflect on the story

Play some quiet music. Give out some dead-looking leaves, large enough to draw on. Ask the children to think of a person or situation that seems hopeless, and write or draw about it on the leaf. Using drawing pins, affix the leaves to a brown felt or wooden cross. Explain that God is a God of life, who can bring life, hope and power where there has been sadness and despair. Give out some fresh green leaves and pin them over the dead ones, as a sign that God can be trusted to bring hope and life out of our prayers.

Alternatively, ask where each person thinks they are in the story, perhaps with drawings of the different stages of the bones' development—for example, scattered bones... coming together gradually... fleshed out but without any breath of God in them... fully alive in body and spirit and ready to be a force for good in the world. Finally, pray that God's breath will fill everyone present.

Death in a family
The story of Jesus and the widow's son

Bible links

Luke 7:11–17

You will need:

A family photograph, a large teardrop shape cut out of card, post-it notes or stickers (two per person), smaller teardrop shapes cut out of card (one per person), pens, paper plates, colouring pens

— The Barnabas Children's Bible —

Story 267

Background to the story

As Jesus travelled around Galilee, telling everyone about God's kingdom, he performed many miracles. Jesus responded with compassion to the many needs he encountered: healing those who were unwell, releasing those who were troubled by evil spirits and, sometimes, even raising people from death. Jesus showed the world that God was a God of life. Only Luke tells us about the time when Jesus encountered a funeral procession in a village called Nain. The dead man was a widow's only son. First she had lost her husband and now her only child had also been taken from her. As she grieved for her son, she also grieved that she had no breadwinner left in the home. Alone in the world, she faced a very grim future.

Jesus had compassion on the widow's situation. Breaking the strict religious laws about touching the dead, Jesus laid his hand on the stretcher, commanding the young man to get up. Immediately, the widow's son came back to life and Jesus returned him to his mother. The story is reminiscent of the account of Elijah bringing a widow's son back to life in 1 Kings 17:17–24, which is why the people who saw Jesus' miracle were full of awe, saying, 'A great prophet is here with us' (Luke 7:16).

Open the story

Cut up a family photograph or picture of a family that includes both adults and children into jigsaw-shaped pieces so that all the people are separated out. Scatter the pieces around the room. The children need to collect all of the pieces and put the jigsaw together.

Talk about family units. Emphasise that some families are very small—maybe just two adults or one adult and one child, or other examples suitable for the age of the children you are working with. Other families could be very large units. In a church, we often talk about the people who belong to the church as being part of a family—God's family.

Take an adult out of the completed jigsaw picture. Ask the children what happens when one person is taken out of the picture. How does this change the family unit? Is it still a family? Be open to what the children may offer.

Take a child out of the picture. Ask the children what happens when a second person is taken out. How might the others in the picture feel if two of their family were missing?

In this activity, take care to be sensitive to those who may have specific family issues.

Tell the story

Explain that the person in today's story was part of a family. She had a husband and a son. First her husband died and now her only son had died, too. She was left alone.

Read the first part of the story from *The Barnabas Children's Bible* (story 267). Continue until the line where Jesus goes to the widow to comfort her. Pause and ask the children how the woman might be feeling. How might the boy's friends be feeling? How might the other people in his family be feeling? On post-it notes or stickers, ask the children to write down some of their suggested words—for example, sad, lonely, frightened, and so on. Stick the post-it notes or stickers on the large teardrop shape.

Read the rest of the story. Ask the children how the widow might be feeling when her son is brought back to life. How might his friends be feeling? How might his family be feeling? Turn the teardrop over. Repeat the same activity as above, with children writing words on post-it notes or stickers—joyful, happy, amazed, and so on.

Talk about the story

As you turn the teardrop over from the 'sad' side to the 'happy' side', talk about what it means for tears of sadness to become tears of joy. Talk about situations when that may have happened. Allow the children to contribute from their own experiences.

Play with the story

On paper plates, create a gallery of faces that depict the many moods of the story: the tearful widow; her sad friends; Jesus' sympathetic face; the angry faces of the religious leaders (because Jesus touched the stretcher); the surprised disciples; the scared onlookers (because the dead man got up!); the amazed crowds; the overjoyed widow; the stunned young man and so on. If desired, use the gallery to create an improvised puppet show of the story.

Reflect on the story

Invite each person to take a smaller teardrop and think or pray for someone who is sad, or about a sad situation, perhaps someone who is unwell or someone who is sad because a person they love has died. At an appropriate time, turn the teardrop over and invite everyone to pray quietly or say 'thank you' for something that is good or happy—for example, someone who was ill and is now better. Encourage everyone to take their teardrop home and continue to pray for the sad person or situation.

The death of a friend
The story of Lazarus

Bible links

John 11:1–44

You will need:

Different colours that the children can pick up, such as fabrics, squares of felt, paint sample cards or similar

— The Barnabas Children's Bible —

Story 285

Background to the story

Lazarus and his two sisters, Mary and Martha, were good friends of Jesus. It seems that he often stayed at their home in Bethany, near Jerusalem, on his travels. Everyone needs somewhere to go and relax, away from the routines of the day and the pressures of life. This must have been even truer for Jesus, who was so often surrounded by crowds of people demanding his attention or by the religious leaders, out to trap him into saying something incriminating.

Lazarus' home must have been a haven for Jesus, and his relationship with the family would have been a very special one, so the news of Lazarus' illness would have been of great concern. Surely Jesus would have wanted to be with his friend as soon as was practically possible. Instead, we read the strange response that Jesus gives to the news (John 11:15). And it gets worse. Because of the delay, by the time Jesus does arrive, his friend is dead. Mary is inconsolable and Martha is angry because she knows that Jesus could have done something and, indeed, still could.

Jesus' reaction is striking. He starts crying (v. 35) and is terribly upset (the Greek words used here suggest indignation and anger at the ugliness caused by death). God is a God of life and Jesus is expressing God's own outrage at the way death has spoiled his world. Jesus goes on to show the glory of God by calling Lazarus back from death. All this happens only days before

Jesus' own death and resurrection. John clearly wants us to make the connection between this story and the miracle of Easter.

Open the story

Invite the children to talk about their best friends. What makes a best friend… how would they feel if their best friend were ill… how would they want to help? Has anyone ever let his or her best friend down? How much disappointment can true friendship take? Are there some hurts that friendships can't survive? Ask the children where they go when they want to get away for a while. Where do they feel most at home when they want some peace and quiet? Has anyone ever had to say 'no' to a request for help from a friend, because they knew that the friend's request wasn't the best thing for him or her?

Tell the story

Spread out a collection of different coloured fabrics and felts. Talk about the way different colours match different moods and feelings, such as yellow or green for illness, red for anger or blue for sadness. In some countries, the colour people wear at funerals is black, and in other countries it is white. What colour would you choose for death… and for life? Sometimes feelings need more complicated mixtures, and we won't always agree on what these mixtures are.

Tell the story in sections. Jesus was friends with a family. There were two sisters and one brother in the family. The sisters were called Martha and Mary, and the brother was called Lazarus. One day, Lazarus fell ill—very ill. What colour might go with how Lazarus felt? What colour might go with how his sisters felt? The sisters sent for Jesus with a message that Lazarus was dying. How do the children think Jesus felt? Invite them to choose a colour. Yet Jesus stayed where he was.

Jesus waited two whole days before he set out for Bethany. How do the children think the sisters felt when Jesus didn't come? Invite them to choose a colour. By the time Jesus arrived in Bethany, Lazarus had been dead for four days. The sisters had laid his body in a tomb. Ask the children what colour would go with Martha now.

Martha met Jesus and said, 'Lord, if you had been here, my brother would not have died. Yet even now I know that God will do anything you ask.' Jesus said, 'Your brother will live again!' Invite the children to choose a colour that goes with these words.

Jesus then said, 'I am the one who raises the dead to life! Everyone who has faith in me will live, even if they die. And everyone who lives because of faith in me will never really die. Do you believe this?' Martha replied, 'Yes, Lord! I believe you are... the Son of God.' What colour do the children think would go with Martha now?

Martha ran to get Mary, who fell at Jesus' feet, crying, and Jesus also burst into tears. Invite the children to choose a colour that would go with Jesus now. The sisters took Jesus to the tomb. He told them to open up the tomb door. Martha was worried that the body would be smelly. What colour would the children put with Lazarus? Jesus prayed, then called out, 'Lazarus, come out!' Lazarus came out, still wrapped in his burial cloth. What colour would the children put with Lazarus now?

Mary and Martha took Lazarus home, and many people believed in Jesus, though some were angry with him. What colours would the children choose for Mary, Martha and Lazarus now?

Talk about the story

Using the picture from page 252 of *The Barnabas Children's Bible* or a similar picture from another Bible story book, try to recreate the scene, using the children to be the different characters in it. Find out what they might be saying or thinking at the moment shown in the picture. Keeping the same characters, ask the children to make a similar freeze-frame picture of what happened just before this scene and what happened just after it. Then run the three scenes as a short play.

Ask a few questions, such as those below.

- Why do you think Jesus didn't just stop Lazarus dying in the first place?
- Why do you think Jesus burst into tears when he saw Mary crying?
- How does that make you feel about Jesus?
- When Jesus brought Lazarus back from the dead, how do you think Martha and Mary felt?
- What puzzles you about this story?
- What do you like best about this story?
- What do you want to take away to think about?

Play with the story

Pick up on the colours that were chosen when you told the story and invite the children to use the colours to create a joint abstract collage or timeline of colour that represents all the feelings of the story. As an alternative activity, you might like to do the standard 'wrapping a friend up in a toilet roll' for the grave clothes part of the story.

Reflect on the story

Invite the children to plant some seeds. Think about the way the seeds are buried in the ground and then come to life as something completely different and wonderful. Jesus promised that he is the one who raises us to life again. Christians believe that even when we die, like the seed being buried and then growing into something new, Jesus will give us a new, different and wonderful life with him.

Death is not the end

The story of Good Friday and Easter Sunday

Bible links

Luke 23:32–43

You will need:

Two pieces of paper (A3 is best but A4 will also work), each marked with a large red X; one piece of paper, the same size as the others, marked with a large Roman cross (+); heart-shaped post-it notes or paper cut out in heart shapes (two hearts per person); sticky-tack; a range of craft materials, including air-drying clay

— The Barnabas Children's Bible —

Stories 308–311

Background to the story

In Romans 5:12–19, Paul writes that death came into the world because of one man's disobedience, but the gift of new life has come through the one man, Jesus Christ, who perfectly obeyed God. Mysteriously, the cross was planned from the beginning as the only way to reverse the disastrous effects of our turning away from God. This new life could only come through Jesus' death, which is why Paul also writes that finally, because of Easter, death will be swallowed up in victory (1 Corinthians 15:54–56).

For Christians, the events of Good Friday and Easter Day stand at the turning point of the history of the universe. Because of what Jesus did, everything has changed. Death no longer has the last word: it is just the beginning of a life that goes on for ever.

Open the story

Place one sheet of paper marked with a red X on the floor. Ask the children what this sign means if they see it on their school work. It means they have made a mistake. Can anyone remember a time at school when they got something wrong? Can anyone remember a time when they tried their best at something and still got it wrong? How did that feel? If anyone says they have never got things wrong, ask them how they might feel if they did. How does it make you feel inside when you get things wrong? Explain that we all do things wrong, adults as well as children, and we need to be honest with ourselves and others when that happens.

Place the second sheet of paper marked with a red X on the floor. Ask the children what this sign means if you see it underneath someone's name on a birthday card. It means love: that person loves you. Can the children remember a time when someone really special said that they loved them or sent a card with that sign on it? How did they feel (to avoid embarrassment, the children can keep their thoughts to themselves if they prefer). Explain that we all need to know, deep inside, that we are loved by others.

Tell the story

Introduce the story by explaining that Jesus had done nothing wrong, yet some people wanted him to be killed. He was arrested and taken to a place called Golgotha or 'the Place of the Skull'. As he walked through the streets, some people shouted unkind things. Others cried as he walked by because it made them so sad. Jesus was nailed to a cross. On either side of him was a thief. They, too, were to be put to death, but Jesus was the one who had done nothing wrong. Again, some people shouted unkind things at Jesus when he was on the cross. Others cried because they were so sad. At around three o'clock in the afternoon, Jesus called out, 'It is finished' and he died.

Pause and talk about the story so far. Ask a willing volunteer to take the place of someone in the crowd who didn't want Jesus to die. How do they feel, watching Jesus being put to death? Do they think they should stand up for Jesus and shout out to save him? Why might they not want to do that?

Continue with the story by explaining that Jesus' body was taken from the cross, wrapped in strips of linen and placed in a tomb, which was sealed by a large, very heavy stone. If you wish, read story 311, 'The empty tomb', from *The Barnabas Children's Bible*.

Talk about the story

Ask a willing volunteer to take the place of the thief who was kind to Jesus. How do they feel, knowing that they have done wrong but Jesus has done nothing wrong and is going to die? Next, ask someone to be Pilate. How does it feel to have made the decision to put Jesus to death when Jesus hadn't done anything wrong? How does Pilate feel as Jesus dies?

Place the sheet of paper with a Roman cross marked on it on the floor between the two red crosses. Remind the children that the X cross says, 'You have done wrong' but also says, 'I love you'. Point to the Roman cross and say, 'We all do things wrong, but Jesus died on a cross so that we can be forgiven. He did that because he loves us so much.'

Play with the story

The cross is the central symbol of the Christian faith, recognised and used all over the world. It is a shape that reminds us that God is a God of life. Because of the cross, death has been turned upside down. Christians from many different countries have designed and made their own crosses from local materials and from within their own cultures to express the importance of the cross in their lives. There are many examples of crosses in *A-cross the World* (Barnabas, 2005), with accompanying ideas for craft activities. Provide a range of craft materials, including air-drying clay, and invite the children to design, create and decorate their own special cross.

Reflect on the story

Give each person two heart-shaped post-it notes (or two paper hearts) and a small piece of sticky tack. Play some quiet music and invite everyone to find their own space in the room. On one heart, ask the children to write or draw something they have done wrong or something they want to say 'sorry' for. Next, ask them to stick the other heart over the top so that no one can see what they have written.

When the children are ready, gather in a circle. Place the paper with the Roman cross in the centre. Invite the children to stick their hearts on to the cross with a piece of sticky tack and quietly say, 'Please forgive me', 'Thank you that you died for me', 'Thank you that you love me' or something similar.

— Theme 5 —

Depths and heights

Season: Easter to Pentecost

General introduction to the theme

The big story of the Bible tracks the progress of God's people from deep places of despair through to mountain-top experiences of joy. The spiritual journey from depths to heights is also reflected in the geography of the landscape. Similarly, the journey from slavery in Egypt to freedom in the promised land moves from the river valley of the Nile, via the thunderous summit of Sinai, to the safety of Mount Zion. The reverse is also true: the tragedy of the exile sees God's people led from the familiar mountains of Judah down to the lowland plains of Babylon.

In the New Testament, John the Baptist declares that before God's promised Messiah comes, every valley should be filled up and every mountain and hill levelled (Luke 3:5). God's kingdom is going to turn the traditional order of things upside down. At the beginning of his ministry, it is from a hillside that Jesus pronounces a blessing on all those who find themselves at the bottom of the heap, while later it is on a mountain that three of his disciples catch a glimpse of heaven. Finally, the story tells us that Jesus had to 'go up' to Jerusalem, where his death on a hill outside the city was the only way to fulfil the words first sung by Mary, namely that her son would 'drag strong rulers from their thrones and put humble people in places of power' (Luke 1:52).

This theme is traced across the Bible in the lives of individuals who experienced rescue from the depths, and also some of the events in the heights that helped shape the Church. God can be found both in heights and in depths (Psalm 139:7–8), and therefore we can be sure that nothing can separate us from God's love: 'neither death, nor life... nor height, nor depth, nor anything else in all creation' (Romans 8:38–39, RSV).

Reflective overview

A Bible, three circles of cloth (dark blue, blue and light blue), two cardboard cylinders (one smaller than the other), a piece of rope, a model crown or throne, a wavy piece of very dark blue cloth, a model of a large fish, a manger, small circles of light blue cloth, a tealight candle, a circle of dark blue cloth, a cross, white feathers

Bible story: Psalm 139:7–8

Action: *Open up the Bible and then lay it down at your side.*

Script: God has given us the stories in his book to show us what he is like and how he works in our lives.

Action: *Set out a circular base cloth of dark blue. Place a cylinder at the centre and cover it with another circle of lighter blue so that it looks like a hill with a wide flat top. Place a smaller cylinder on top of this and cover it with a circle of pale blue to make a sort of wedding cake effect.*

Script: Our world has low places and high places. We sometimes feel low and we sometimes feel high. God has work to do in the depths and in the heights, so the Bible has stories of low places and high places.

Action: *Move your hands from the base to the summit as you speak, and then from the summit to the base as you say the words from Psalm 139. Repeat this action every time you say these words.*

Script: Where could I go to escape from your Spirit? If I go up to the heavens you are there; if I make my bed in the depths, you are there.

Bible story: Jeremiah 38:1–27

Action: *On the dark blue base, place a rope for Jeremiah so that everyone can see it clearly.*

Script: Sometimes God's people go to a low place. There was once a man called Jeremiah. His enemies threw him down a well, where he started to sink into the mud. But his friends used a rope to rescue him and he was then allowed to speak God's words to the high king.

Bible story: Esther 1:1–10

Script: Where could I go to escape from your Spirit? If I go up to the heavens you are there; if I make my bed in the depths, you are there.

Action: *Place a throne or crown on the middle tier of the hill, where everyone can see it.*

Script: God puts people in high places, too. There was once a young woman called Esther. She was made high queen so that she could save God's people in a time of danger.

Bible story: Jonah 1:1 — 2:10

Script: Where could I go to escape from your Spirit? If I go up to the heavens you are there; if I make my bed in the depths, you are there.

Action: *Place a very dark blue, wavy shape on the lowest base cloth, to represent the sea, and place a fish in this dark area.*

Script: Where could be a lower place than the bottom of the sea? There was once a man called Jonah. He was thrown overboard and sank to the very depths of the sea. But God sent a great fish to save him and bring him back up to dry land.

Bible story: Luke 2:1–7

Script: Where could I go to escape from your Spirit? If I go up to the heavens you are there; if I make my bed in the depths, you are there.

Action: *Place a manger on the base cloth. Move your hand back up the mountain to show the transformation Jesus brings.*

Script: Jesus knew all about low places and high places. He came down to earth from highest heaven. He was born in a down-to-earth stable. When he grew up, he lived among down-to-earth people—and he changed them. He turned low places to high places wherever he went.

Bible story: Matthew 5:1–12

Action: *Place several small circles of pale blue on the middle blue cloth so that everyone can see them.*

Script: Once, Jesus went up a hill to teach people about his Father's kingdom. He told them that God blesses those who depend on him, and those who are humble he raises up. God's kingdom turns everything upside down and inside out.

Bible story: Matthew 17:1–8

Action: *Place a tealight candle on the middle tier of the hill. Light it as you say the following words.*

Script: Once, Jesus took three of his friends up a high mountain. There they caught a glimpse of how wonderful Jesus was, when his clothes shone with the light of highest heaven.

Bible story: Acts 2:1–4

Action: *Place a circle of dark blue on the very top tier of the hill and place a cross on it. Movements of the hand should illustrate the heights and depths in the words that follow.*

Script: Jesus turned a high place to the lowest place of all when he was lifted up on a cross to die, then was buried deep in a tomb. But then he turned that lowest place to the highest place when he rose up again.

Action: *Gently let white feathers fall over the whole set.*

Script: Jesus' Spirit came down from a high place like a dove to rest on God's people, so that now anyone can have Jesus close to them, whether we are in a low place or a high place.

Script: Where could I go to escape from your Spirit? If I go up to the heavens you are there; if I make my bed in the depths, you are there.
      I wonder what low places you know…
      I wonder what high places you know…
      I wonder where you feel closest to God…
      I wonder why God lets us go down to the depths…
      I wonder what it feels like in the heights…
      I wonder whether you would be prepared to go to a low place or a high place for God…

From the depths of a well
The story of Jeremiah

Bible link

Jeremiah 37—38

You will need:

A range of colourful 3D and tactile materials

— The Barnabas Children's Bible —

Story 211 (NB: It would be helpful also to read the surrounding stories about Jeremiah, especially stories 207–212, to put the events into context)

Background to the story

While he was still very young, Jeremiah was chosen by God to be a prophet. He went on to speak out for God during the reigns of the last five kings of Judah. Caught between the two great superpowers of the day, Egypt and Babylon, the people had turned to worshipping idols as 'additional security' in dangerous times. This had led them to desert the one true God and his laws. Jeremiah's uncompromising preaching against idolatry led to much opposition and, for him, times of loneliness and even despair. He writes, 'I have told the people that you, Lord, will punish them, but they just laugh and refuse to listen' (Jeremiah 6:10).

During the reign of Zedekiah, the last king, Jeremiah was a lone voice, though secretly the king still respected what he had to say. Nevertheless, Jeremiah was accused of betraying his country with his talk of an inevitable defeat, and he was imprisoned. Later, angry officials wanted him punished as a traitor and he was thrown down a deep, muddy well and left to die.

It was a foreigner from Ethiopia who dared to approach the king and arrange Jeremiah's rescue but, even so, the prophet continued under lock and key during the long final siege of Jerusalem. The siege ended with the burning of the city, and the king and leading people were taken into exile. Even Jeremiah was led away in chains but was then released and allowed to stay in Judah because a kindly Babylonian guard recognised that he had been speaking the truth from God. Jeremiah's Ethiopian rescuer was also saved.

Open the story

Jeremiah faced constant harassment and hardship during his years as a prophet. He must have felt like giving up, so many times. Perhaps the memory of the day when he first heard God speaking to him kept him going. Read Jeremiah 1:1–19. You could use the retelling from *The Barnabas Children's Bible* (story 204). Jeremiah thought he was too young for the job and not a good speaker, but God promised to help him (vv. 4–9). The message would be a hard one but, again, God promised to protect him to the end (vv. 10, 19).

Talk about what special memories or experiences the children may have had that gave them strength to keep going when things were tough. Has anyone had the experience of knowing just the right words to say when put on the spot? Jesus promises that he will be with us and give us the right words to say (Matthew 28:20; Luke 21:14–15).

Tell the story

Summarise the story in Jeremiah 37 and 38, using the simple sentences below. Encourage the children to respond to each line as good news (cheers) or bad news (boos), sad news (ah!) or courageous news (hurray!).

- Jerusalem is being attacked by the Babylonians…
- They say the Egyptians are coming to the rescue…
- Jeremiah says the Babylonians will be back…
- The king says it's all going to be OK…
- Jeremiah says that the king is wrong and must surrender…
- The king asks Jeremiah to pray for the city…
- Jeremiah refuses to give false hope…
- Jeremiah is put in an underground prison…
- The king treats Jeremiah more kindly by putting him in a ground-level prison…
- The king's advisers want Jeremiah dead…

- The king doesn't stop them…
- Jeremiah is thrown down a muddy well to die…
- Ebedmelech from Ethiopia dares to talk to the king….
- He organises Jeremiah's rescue with ropes…
- The king talks to Jeremiah in secret…
- The king refuses to surrender and save lives…
- Jeremiah is put back in prison…
- The siege of Jerusalem continues for one and a half years…
- The city falls and is burned to the ground…
- The king is captured and, with the leading citizens, is taken to Babylon…
- Jeremiah is led off in chains…
- But he is released by a kind guard and allowed to go home…
- God looked after Jeremiah, just as he had promised…

Talk about the story

Jeremiah stuck to the message that God gave him to speak, even though he was bullied again and again to keep him quiet. Before being put down the well, Jeremiah had already been lied about, banned from the temple and threatened with death. His written prophecies had been cut up and burnt, and he had been physically attacked. His fellow prophet, Uriah, had been murdered. No wonder he was tempted to despair and give up (15:10).

It is hard when no one believes we are telling the truth, or when we are the only ones who think differently and won't just go along with the majority opinion. Bullies deal in lies and threats.

Explore with the children what their breaking point is. Could they have put up with all that happened to Jeremiah and still have trusted God? What advice for coping with bullies can they suggest? What helped Jeremiah not to give up and go home?

Play with the story

Jeremiah was drawn up from the depths to the heights by a kind stranger. Sometimes, God's help comes from unexpected places. A rope lowered by one of the king's officials (someone who was not even originally from Judah) must have really taken Jeremiah by surprise. Make individual or group collages depicting this memorable moment, using a variety of different tactile materials and fabric for the mud at the bottom of the well, the brick work of the well itself, the rope that was lowered, Jeremiah's ruined clothes and his rescuer's smart robes.

Reflect on the story

Jeremiah's message wasn't all doom and gloom. He also promised the people that one day they would return to their country from exile. He even bought a plot of land himself during the fighting, as a sign that his promise would come true one day (Jeremiah 32:1–15). He passed on God's words about a new covenant (31:31–34) and also the promise, 'I will bless you with a future filled with hope' (29:11).

Write or print out the ten words of Jeremiah 29:11 on separate pieces of card and place them face down. Ask everyone to think of a situation in which someone may be facing 'the depths' for some reason (it might be someone in the group). Suggest a few situations of your own to get everyone thinking. In a time of quiet, invite the children, one at a time, to turn over a card until all the cards are face up. Rearrange the words to make the verse, which is God's promise to us today.

From the heights of a throne
The story of Queen Esther

Bible links

The book of Esther

You will need:

Large sheets of paper, newspaper, bin bags or similar; sticky tape, scissors, paper and pens, dice (one for every three children), Bibles, a toy sceptre, perfume, scroll, grapes, plastic pots and dried peas, ingredients to make sweet pastries (see below), pictures from mission and aid magazines

— The Barnabas Children's Bible —

Stories 227–231

Background to the story

The story of Esther is set in the time of the Jewish exile. Esther was a Jewish orphan who was the adopted daughter of Mordecai. She caught the eye of the king of Persia, King Xerxes, and became his new queen. Esther kept quiet about her nationality and, as queen, earned the king's respect when she and Mordecai warned him of plots against his life.

When Haman became prime minister, second in power to the king, he demanded that everyone should bow to him, but Mordecai refused. As a result, Haman won permission to have all the Jews killed. Esther intervened on behalf of her people, first reminding the king at a party of how she and Mordecai had saved his life and later, at a subsequent party, exposing Haman's plan. Haman was hanged but the edict to kill the Jews could not be revoked. The king gave the Jews permission to defend themselves against the attacks on their lives. The festival of Purim is celebrated annually to commemorate this event.

The story of Esther is unique in that it doesn't ever directly mention God. However, it is clear that God is watching over all that happens at every stage of the story. God uses Esther's favoured position to make her the right person, in the right place, at the right time, to save God's people from destruction. Even so, Esther had to have the courage to speak out to save her people. God didn't force her to speak. It was a brave move, for in those days no woman, not even one as highly placed as Esther, could speak to the king unless he spoke to her first.

Open the story

Split the children into teams of three and hold a five-minute fashion contest to dress one person from each team in an outfit made out of paper, using only scissors and tape to help. Invite the models, wearing the finished garments, to strut along a catwalk while another member of their team does a suitably over-the-top commentary ('And now we have Julie wearing a natty little number in yesterday's *Express*, held together with sticky tape…'). Comment on how gorgeous they all look.

Next, play a version of a beetle drive to create a beautiful female face. Explain that the numbers on the dice stand for the following.

1. head and neck
2. eyes
3. nose and ears
4. mouth
5. hair
6. jewellery

In their teams, the children take turns to throw the dice. The first person to throw a 1 can draw the head and neck. The next person to throw a 2 can add the eyes and so on. No one can throw the dice while the previous person is drawing. The face must be completed in the right order. The first team to complete the face wins. When all the faces are completed, hold a second competition to see which team has drawn the most beautiful face. Finally, explain that today's story is about someone whose beauty put her in a very special position.

Tell the story

Use the notes below to tell the story of Esther in your own words. Hand out Bibles and encourage the children to find the book of Esther. Ask some of the older children to read out the verses as marked. Suggestions for possible visual aids are included, to be used with the story. The story is set in Persia, in the city of Susa, about 500 years before Jesus' birth. King Xerxes (pronounced Zerkzees) was an incredibly powerful man: he had the power to chop off someone's head just for sneezing at the wrong time.

Show the children the sceptre. Explain that if someone went to see King Xerxes when they hadn't been invited, he might refuse to hold out his golden sceptre (demonstrate), and then that person would be killed straight away. If he held it out (demonstrate), it meant that he was pleased and the person could speak to him. He was a very, very scary man indeed!

King Xerxes quarrelled with his first wife and was looking for another queen. He held a beauty contest to decide whom he would marry. The most beautiful girl was Esther. She had to spend a whole year going through beauty therapy, and after that she was crowned as queen.

Pass some perfume round for the children to sniff and spray. Esther was one of God's people, a Jew, but the king didn't know that. She was an orphan and had been brought up by her grown-up cousin, Mordecai. One day, Mordecai happened to overhear some men plotting to kill the king. He got a message to Queen Esther, she told the king and the king's life was saved. Mordecai's good deed was written down in the royal records.

Pass round a scroll and continue with the story by saying that Mordecai refused to bow to anyone but God. So when Prime Minister Haman demanded that everyone should bow down to him, Mordecai refused. This made Haman very angry. He decided to take revenge on Mordecai by tricking the king into having all the Jews in the kingdom killed.

(Read Esther 3:8)

The king let Haman send out a proclamation.

(Read 3:13)

How do you think the Jews felt? Mordecai got a message to Esther…

(Read 4:8)

Esther panicked…

(Read 4:11)

Mordecai was firm…

(Read 4:13–14)

Esther decided she had to be brave…

(Read 4:16)

Trembling, Esther went to the king. Remember, if he didn't hold out his sceptre… Pick up the sceptre and tell the children that the king held the sceptre out to his queen. He asked her what she wanted and she invited him to a feast that night. Pass round some grapes and tell how Esther threw such a good party for the king that he invited her to ask for anything she wanted. But Esther knew she had to go carefully. She invited the king to come to another party and to bring Prime Minister Haman with him. That night, the king couldn't sleep, so he got a servant to read out the royal records to him. When the king was reminded about how Mordecai had saved his life he asked…

(Read 6:3)

So he asked Haman…

(Read 6:6)

Haman was already delighted that he'd been invited to the queen's party, so he thought the king wanted to honour him. He said…

(Read 6:7–9)

And the king replied…

(Read 6:10)

How might Haman have felt? He had a gallows built in the courtyard to hang Mordecai on the next day. At the second party, the king asked Esther what she wanted more than anything. She replied…

(Read 7:3–4)

The king was horrified and asked who this evil man was. Esther replied…

(Read 7:6)

The king was so upset that he had Haman hanged on his own gallows and made Mordecai prime minister instead. Although the king couldn't change the proclamation about the Jews, he did say that they could defend themselves and fight back if they were attacked.

Sadly, there was much bloodshed and many people were slaughtered, but the lives of the Jews were saved. Even today, Jewish people remember Esther's bravery and God's rescue, at the festival of Purim.

Talk about the story

Use some of the questions below to talk about the story.

- I wonder if Esther enjoyed being queen…
- I wonder what it was like being the only person who believed in God in the palace…
- I wonder if you're ever been in a place like that…
- I wonder what was the hardest moment for Esther…
- I wonder if you've ever had to be brave to help someone else…
- I wonder where you can see God at work in the story of Esther…
- I wonder if God has put you where you are for a reason…

Arrange the children in two lines opposite each other. Set up the dilemma that Esther found herself in when she heard what was going to happen to the Jews, and after she had spoken with Mordecai. What should she do? Choose someone to be Esther. As the volunteer walks slowly down the alley, the people on either side become the voices of Esther's conscience and suggest what she should do next. For example, they might encourage her to ignore the danger. After all, she was comfortably off and wouldn't have been in danger… But Esther owed it to Mordecai, who had adopted her, to do something to help… But what if the king refused to see her or listen to what she had to say? Encourage the children to stay in role in order to bring the story alive and connect it to issues of conscience facing us today. Use the same technique with other characters in the story to explore their feelings and motivations.

Play with the story

Whenever Haman's name is read out in the Esther story, it is traditional to blot it out by making as loud a noise as possible—booing, hissing and shaking 'greggers' (noise makers). Make some greggers from a variety of plastic containers filled with dried peas, pebbles or lentils. Decorate the greggers with coloured paper and ribbons.

Eating triangular pastries with sweet fillings (known as Hamantaschen) is one of the treats at the festival of Purim. You will need some homemade or frozen shortcrust pastry and assorted fillings. Traditional fillings include honey, poppy seeds and plum jam, but you could also use mincemeat.

Roll the pastry thinly and cut out circles. Pour a spoonful of filling into the centre and lift the sides to make a three-cornered shape. Seal the edges with water. Transfer to a greased baking tray and bake for about ten minutes at Gas Mark 5 (180°C). Make sure you leave enough time for the pastries to cool before eating them, as the filling will be very hot.

Find out more about the Jewish festival of Purim. When does it take place? What does 'Purim' mean? If possible, invite someone from the Jewish tradition to your group and ask them about the festival.

Reflect on the story

Esther was someone who was raised from the depths to the heights when she became queen. In turn, she was later able to rescue her own people from the depths of danger and ensure the survival of her nation.

Many groups of people in the world today face similar oppression. Some are refugees; others are caught up in wars or natural disasters. For some, their rights are not respected by authoritarian and hostile regimes. Collect some pictures from mission and aid magazines. Ask the children to imagine what it must be like to feel so threatened, without any support, a home or security. Ask them to name some of the things they would be sad to lose or have to give up. Read Esther 4:14, then invite the children to listen quietly to God together to hear what he wants them to do to help others who are in deep places of need.

From the depths of the ocean
The story of Jonah

You will need:

Tables and chairs, materials for an undersea collage, a pack of playing cards

— The Barnabas Children's Bible —

Stories 186–190

Background to the story

Jonah was a reluctant missionary who didn't want to be the one who gave a second chance to the people of Nineveh—Israel's cruel and ungodly neighbours. Foolishly, Jonah thought he could run away from God, but the storm at sea soon led the sailors to realise that someone on board had got to go. Once Jonah had been thrown overboard, the storm was stilled and the sailors were safe. Meanwhile, Jonah was also miraculously safe inside the great fish, from where he thought afresh about God's request. Jonah went to Nineveh and the people repented, as Jonah had feared they would. Jonah found it hard to accept that 'outsiders' could be forgiven, and he complained to God. God's generosity was far more than Jonah could stand!

Open the story

Jonah is an example of someone who deliberately chose to run away from God. But running away from God is impossible—it's like trying to escape your own shadow.

Invite each child in turn to think silently of a hiding place somewhere about the premises. It can be as tiny or as impractical as they like but it must be a real place.

The rest of the children are then given 15 questions to try to discover the location of the hiding place: the child being questioned is only allowed to answer 'yes' or 'no'. At the end of this game, read Psalm 139:7–12, where King David reminds himself that nowhere is out of reach of God's love.

Tell the story

Jonah thought that putting as much distance as he could between himself and Nineveh was the way to escape God's request. Use any tables or chairs that you have in your meeting area to make a boat, including a place for Jonah to hide himself away from the crew in its hold. Choose one person to be Jonah while the others become the crew in the middle of the unseasonal and violent storm. Ask them to get into character and feel the story from the inside.

- What is going on in their minds as the storm rages?
- What are their hopes and fears of getting out alive?
- What different actions do they recommend taking?

When something goes badly wrong, it isn't unusual to want to find something or someone to blame. Jonah—the unknown passenger, hiding away below deck—is an obvious target. Hot-seat the crew, asking them, one by one, what they think should be done. There are ideas in the story already, but let the children explore other attitudes that might have arisen. Jonah's response makes it clear that, deep down, he knew all along that he couldn't ever run away from God. He also knew that running away would only make things worse for himself and everyone else.

Set up a conscience circus activity, in which half the group is Jonah's conscience, trying to urge him to do the right thing by the sailors and allow them to throw him overboard, while the other half is Jonah's inner voice, still arguing that he can get away with it and bluff his way out of the situation. Ask one person to represent Jonah. Which voice will he or she follow?

Talk about the story

Jonah's prayer in chapter 2 about his deep-sea experience is one of the literary gems of the Bible. Here he is, in the very depths, crying out to God, who graciously and miraculously brings Jonah back up to the heights again. The prayer is the honest thanksgiving of a person who has been found by God but doesn't expect or deserve God's grace. The experience literally turns Jonah's life around and gives him a second chance.

Talk with the children about what God's grace in the story means in relation to their own lives. Why might God have bothered to go to such great lengths to rescue and restore Jonah? If someone turned his or her back on us as dramatically as Jonah had on God, would we bother about that person again? Can the children give any examples of situations where they felt like giving up on their friends? Have they ever felt that people have given up on them?

Among other things, the story reminds us that none of us is ever too lost as far as God is concerned.

Play with the story

As a way of illustrating the depths out of which Jonah cried, create an undersea collage. Scenes from *Finding Nemo* or *A Shark's Tale* might give some inspiration. Attach speech air-bubbles of parts of Jonah's prayer to the finished piece. The prayer has some great imagery, including swirling waters, seaweed, underwater rock formations and murky depths (Jonah 2:2–9). If there is time, compare Jonah's prayer with David's experience, as expressed in Psalm 40:1–3. Here is someone else who felt in the depths of despair, but was raised up by God.

Reflect on the story

Play a game of pairs, using all the cards numbered 2 to 5 from a pack of playing cards (16 cards in total). Gather in a circle and place the cards face down in the centre. Invite a child to turn a card over. Before he or she begins to search for a pair, pause to think about somebody or a situation where people feel lost in the depths and in need of help. After a moment, invite the child to search for a matching card: it doesn't matter how many cards are tried before a matching card is found. Remind the children that God is looking for us, to raise us to the heights again. Then pause again before the next card search to say 'thank you' that God never gives up looking for people and offering them his love.

Blessings from the hill
The story of God's blessings

Bible links

Matthew 5:1–10

You will need:

Two paper plates (one with a happy face on it and one with a sad face), paper and pens, one more paper plate per child, 16 blank index cards, heart-shaped post-it notes

— The Barnabas Children's Bible —

Story 262

Background to the story

Each blessing in Matthew 5:1–10 is for an unexpected group of people—not rich, famous and powerful people but those who are disadvantaged, sad and humble. Jesus is speaking about those who, in the world's eyes, are in the depths but, in God's kingdom, are raised to the heights. This is the upside-down kingdom in which a true king is a servant and true riches belong to those who are ready to give everything away.

Open the story

Show the children the two paper plates with the happy and sad faces. Ask the children what makes them happy and what makes them sad. List their answers on paper and place the words they have suggested around the relevant paper plate face. Next, introduce the following eight phrases from the Bible passage.

A: Feeling low about yourself.
B: Feeling sad about others.
C: Being ignored and going unnoticed.
D: Feeling empty on the inside.

E: Not getting your own back on someone, even though they deserve it.
F: Missing out on doing some things that you know are wrong but everyone else says are OK.
G: Getting in between two people who are fighting, and ending up by being shouted at by both.
H: Being got at, even when you've done nothing wrong.

Discuss which face matches the phrases and why. Whatever the children decide, continue by placing all the phrases on the happy plate. Explain that Jesus said that all these things are, in fact, reasons to be happy because they bring us nearer to God and God nearer to us. Wherever God is, that is where his kingdom is, and that is the safest place we can ever be.

Tell the story

Read Matthew 5:1–10 in different Bible translations, including THE MESSAGE. Jesus taught about God's way of doing things and many people gathered to listen. Once, Jesus was speaking to a great crowd on a hillside in Galilee. He told the people about what things are like when God is king. He described the sort of lives God's people should lead. Jesus said that we will be happy if we know we need God, happy if we are sad about being far from him and happy if we always put others first. We will be happy if we long for what is good and right, happy if we are kind and say 'no' to all that is bad, and happy if we are people who make peace. Others might think we are crazy and laugh at us, but this is the only way to be truly happy and make God happy too.

What do the children think will make God really happy? Briefly discuss their ideas and then, on some heart-shaped post-it notes, invite them to write or draw their thoughts.

Talk about the story

Jesus' teaching about what God values turns upside down most people's ideas about what brings true happiness. What do the children think about the statements? Is Jesus really being practical? Has anybody ever really lived out the sort of values Jesus is suggesting? Which of the values is most important?

Play with the story

Look again at the eight key phrases. Why is God close to people who feel like this or express these things? Read Matthew 5:1–10 and encourage the children to link the phrases to the first part of each verse. Ask what God's upside-down kingdom promises to people who feel this way and then lay out eight paraphrase versions of the second part of each verse (see below). Ask the children to link the first set of phrases with the second set.

A: You will be where God is.
B: God will be very close to you.
C: God has big plans for you.
D: God will give you all you really need.
E: God's love will seem more and more real to you.
F: God will be right there for you.
G: God will treat you as family.
H: You are definitely the right way up and in God's place!

Give each child a paper plate on which to draw his or her own happy face and write words to create a set of blessings, based on the ideas that have been shared.

Reflect on the story

In God's amazing kingdom, things look upside down to most of us. For example, those who are first end up being last; those who are weak can end up being strong; those who are lost, least and last are the most important. Perhaps God's kingdom is, in fact, the right way up and it is the world that is upside down!

Use the eight paraphrases of God's blessings as a focus for prayer. Ask the children to think of people they know who are in the depths described by the first part of each blessing. As a way of asking for God's help in the situations, encourage the children to pause and pray silently or out loud before saying the words of comfort that go with each blessing.

Glory on the mountain
The story of the transfiguration

Bible links

Matthew 17:1–9; Mark 9:2–13; Luke 9:28–36

You will need:

A pair of walking boots, liquid wash, a small tent (in its bag), a pair of binoculars, a picture or model of Dr Who's Tardis

— The Barnabas Children's Bible —

Story 278

Background to the story

The transfiguration was certainly a very strange experience for Peter, James and John, who never forgot what they saw up on the mountain. Many years later, Peter wrote about the experience (2 Peter 1:16–18). It is uncertain which mountain it was that Jesus took his friends to, but the story takes place soon after the time when Jesus asked his disciples who they thought he was, at a location near Caesarea Philippi. It is therefore reasonable to assume that the transfiguration probably happened on the nearby Mount Hermon.

Open the story

Explain to the children that they will need to get their imaginations working for today's story, and then introduce the following objects to see if they can find what links them together: climbing boots, liquid wash, a tent in its bag, a pair of binoculars and a picture or model of Dr Who's Tardis. Invite some imaginative connections, but tell the story before giving any answers.

The children also need to get their emotions engaged for the story. Play a simple drama warm-up game to step into the feelings of the event, by inviting the children to stand and face outwards, looking at the walls. Explain that on the count of three, they are going to turn inwards and become statues expressing certain feelings or in the process of doing an action. The story is one of high drama and with big emotions, so the statues they are to make are struggling to walk; being excited; feeling embarrassed; looking surprised; looking very puzzled; being extremely tired; feeling very cold; trying to eavesdrop on a conversation; being frightened to death; feeling dazed and shocked.

Tell the story

Now that the children's imaginations have been released and the feelings of the story have been explored, explain that it's time to go for a walk. This is not just any old walk—not an afternoon stroll along the *(mention the name of a local walk or beauty spot)*. It's a proper walk—in fact, a climb. Ask them if they have brought their walking boots with them and link this idea to the climbing boots that you've displayed. Say that they need to climb a mountain, and not an easy one. This mountain is three times the height of the highest mountains in Britain. Are they up to the task? This mountain has snow on its top. Are they equipped? Have they got snowboards or skis? From the top, you can look down over several countries at the same time. Are they ready for the views? Have they a head for heights? *(Make a link to the binoculars.)*

Explain that the mountain in the story is Mount Hermon in the north of Galilee—the land where Jesus lived. Invite everyone to mime putting on their rucksacks and their boots, and having their walking sticks at the ready. Start walking on the spot to mime the journey upwards. Invite the children to imagine they are following a small group of climbers who are on the path just ahead. There's one, two, three… four of them.

The children recognise the group of three: they are close friends of Jesus, those who are closest to him in his little band. There's Peter and there are the two 'thunder' brothers, James and John—they are always arguing! Peter's a bit of a hot-head at times, but Jesus sees what they can be. He has chosen them for his team and he's asked them to come on this climb.

Encourage heavier footfalls as the children 'climb'. It's hard work. Encourage them to keep up. Wonder together why Jesus and his friends are climbing the mountain. Why does anyone climb a mountain? *(Ask for some suggestions.)* Perhaps we climb mountains just because they are there, or to enjoy the view... or perhaps we want to collect some snow. Explain that people did collect the snow on Mount Hermon so that they could use it to keep food chilled and fresh—a sort of first century version of a fridge. But these four aren't carrying anything to collect snow in. Perhaps they want to get away from it all, to find a bit of peace and quiet? Mount Hermon was well known for that. There were many little shrines in the rocks on its slopes, dedicated to different gods. It was known as the holy mountain.

Encourage heavier and slower footsteps. Invite the children to imagine that the path is getting steeper and narrower. Jesus and his friends are still ahead. Perhaps Jesus is looking for a place to pray and he has invited his three friends to join him. What a long way to go to pray! And so high up! Jesus prayed anywhere, his friends all knew that. Prayer was part of his whole life. He prayed on a boat, by the lake, in the streets, in people's homes, but it wasn't going to be like that today. Today it had to be mountain-top prayer. Wonder together what people think when they go on a long walk or for a climb. What goes through their minds? *(Ask for some suggestions.)*

Explain that James, John and especially Peter had a lot on their minds. A week earlier, Jesus had come out with a surprising question: he was always saying surprising things. He had asked his friends who people thought he was. Jesus was very well known at that time and opinions about him were divided, just as they are today. Some people thought he was a prophet like those of the olden days, perhaps even Elijah. Some people thought that Elijah had never died and that Jesus was perhaps Elijah come back from the past. Others thought Jesus was a reincarnation of John the Baptist, who had died quite recently. People were very superstitious, just as they are today.

Then Jesus paused before asking his friends, 'But who do *you* say I am?' No one dared answer for a while. What if they said the wrong thing? It was Peter who eventually spoke up: 'You're the Messiah, the Son of the living God.' There was another pause and then Jesus smiled. Yes, Peter had got it right. Jesus was the one they'd been waiting for, the one who would kick out the occupying Roman army, the one who would make Israel great again, the one who would reign in Jerusalem as king for ever. Rock on, Peter! In fact, Jesus actually called Peter a rock—a rock on which Jesus' Church would be built. Peter would be the key to what would happen later.

Then Jesus started talking about Jerusalem and being arrested; about being tried and tortured, and about being killed and rising again. Peter was shocked. How could this be right? Jesus knew that Peter hadn't understood: he was thinking about Jesus in the way that everyone else did. He hadn't understood the bigger picture of God's plan. Peter the rock became Peter the devil in one conversation! No wonder Peter had a lot to think about as he climbed with the others. It was the climb of their lives.

Encourage the children to become slow and weary as they climb. It's getting hard work but they are almost there. Ahead, Jesus is looking for a place to pray and his friends are looking for a place to sleep because they are so exhausted. Jesus' friends curl up against some rocks and go to sleep while Jesus goes ahead. He stands and prays with his hands in the air, while they put their heads down and doze off. Encourage the children to stop climbing and watch.

Suddenly Jesus' friends wake up. They can hear voices. Listen! Jesus is talking to someone. Peter, James and John open their eyes but then shut them again because of the glow. No, more than a glow. It's a burning light coming from... or is it through... Jesus. Jesus is transformed by a light. He shines like the sun, bright enough to light up the whole world. The three friends have never seen anything like it. Nothing on earth could ever wash whiter than this. It's dazzling! *(Make a link to the washing liquid.)*

Jesus is the special one from God. They can see it clearly now. He is letting heaven shine in and through him. Heaven always shines through him but suddenly it is more obvious. Suddenly the friends see that there are two other people with Jesus. These people didn't climb the mountain with them. They've come from another place and another time. The friends recognise them as the two great Old Testament characters, Moses and Elijah. Jesus is there in time but out of time; he is in the present but also in the past. *(Make a link to the Tardis.)* Jesus is in heaven but also on earth. His three friends can see it with their own eyes and they can hear Jesus, Moses and Elijah talking about Jerusalem, about how the journey will end and about what will happen next. It's the same thing that Jesus said to Peter about his death—about how he will die and rise again.

Peter wants to hold on to this amazing moment. He thinks about the little shrines he's seen further down the mountain and he calls out, 'Let me make a shelter for each of you, so you can stay here and talk as long as you like.' *(Make a link to the tent.)* But it's then that the cloud comes down—not any old cloud, but a shining, bright cloud. The three friends are terrified. They wrap themselves in their cloaks and shake with fear. Then, just as Moses heard God's voice on Mount Sinai, giving him the ten best ways to live, and just as Elijah heard the gentle whisper of God's voice on Mount Horeb, bringing him into God's presence in a time of need, they too hear God's voice on Mount Hermon: 'This is my own dear Son, and I am pleased with him. Listen to what he says.' When the three friends hear the voice, they are so frightened that they fall flat on the ground. Then Peter feels a hand on his shoulder. It's Jesus—just Jesus—and Jesus is smiling.

Tell the children that it's time to go back down the mountain. The descent is easier, but things have changed. They can never be the same again. Jesus doesn't want his friends to say anything about what happened—not yet, but they will never forget.

Talk about the story

Finish the mime and bring the children back into the present. Talk about what they thought and felt as the story unfolded. Using the props, briefly recap the story.

Play with the story

Find a picture of the transfiguration on the internet or in a library and make black and white copies for each person. Invite the children to add the colours that they think best express the mystery of the scene, and also to add thought bubbles to explore what the different people in the picture are thinking.

Reflect on the story

The transfiguration is a turning point in Jesus' story. Explore what the story means by setting out a focus table with objects that are reminiscent of different parts of the story. On a green felt cloth, place three small figures for the disciples, some prayer hands, a rock for Mount Hermon, a figure of Jesus or an icon based on the story, two figures for Elijah and Moses, and a cross. Ask the children which part of the story they like best. Which part do they think is the most important part? Which part of the story is especially for them today?

Explain that we all have moments when we know there's more to life than what we can see, hear, touch, feel and smell. We have moments of wonder and amazement, glimpses of the big beyond, moments that we can't hold on to. Peter, James and John had a glimpse of the beyond on the mountain, and it was Jesus who opened the door to it. Jesus is the link between the bigger meaning of life and the life that we have here. They belong together and Jesus brings them together. Jesus is the door. He links past, present and future and he links us to God.

Ask the children to think about what they will remember about the story in one hour's time, a day's time, during the week, and for the rest of their lives. End with a time of silence and a simple prayer.

Power from on high
The story of Pentecost

Bible links

Acts 2:1–4

You will need:

A small birthday cake with some candles, a large sheet of paper with a wide border drawn around the edge and five circles drawn inside the border, coloured pens, ribbons, large pieces of card, items for the prayer ideas you choose (see below)

— The Barnabas Children's Bible —

Stories 317 and 319

Background to the story

Pentecost celebrates the birthday of the Church, the day when Jesus fulfilled his promise to send the Spirit of God to be with and in his followers. God's coming as the Holy Spirit was marked by sounds and signs of God's power, a power that enabled Jesus' friends to take the good news about Jesus to the whole world. Jesus had told his followers, 'I will send you the one my Father has promised, but you must stay in the city until you are given power from heaven' (Luke 24:49).

God's Spirit still empowers Christians today to share and show God's love and bring people into his kingdom. This promise is for everyone and every generation (Acts 2:17–18, 39).

Open the story

Introduce the story by producing a birthday cake with a small number of candles. Make connections to the children's own birthdays. Then explain that today's story celebrates a birthday, but there should be over 1980 candles on the cake. The story is about Pentecost, the birthday of the Church. Explain that Pentecost was the day when the Church was filled with God's power.

To illustrate this, introduce the power that is present in a clockwork toy. Ask the children to move round the room as:

- A person and then a robot.
- A real rabbit, then a clockwork rabbit.
- A real ballerina, then a toybox ballerina.
- A soldier, then a clockwork soldier.

Point out that a clockwork toy winds down slowly until it finally stops. Talk about what you'd need to do to make it work again. Pretend to 'wind' some of the children up and set them moving again. Ask one child to perform the task of keeping the others on the move by rushing from one to the other to 'wind them up'. Finish the game and then ask the children to get into groups of four or five. In their groups, ask them to create the sound effects of selected objects, such as a washing machine, vacuum cleaner, lawn mower, car, windmill or firework. Ask them to demonstrate what happens when the item is plugged in and switched on. What happens when the power fails?

Tell the story

As you tell the story of Pentecost, invite the children to add drawings to the large sheet of paper you have prepared. Explain that it was the festival of Shavuot or Pentecost—a time when Jewish people would come to Jerusalem from all over the world to celebrate together.

Inside the border on the paper, draw adults and children of all ethnic groups and colours, smiling and running in towards the centre. The people were celebrating their harvest festival, the time when they would offer the first of their crops to God and decorate their houses with flowers—much as we do in church at harvest time today.

In one circle, invite the children to draw as many sorts of fruits, vegetables and grains as they can think of. Explain that Shavuot was also the festival to celebrate the time when God gave Moses the Ten Commandments. Find out how many of the commandments the children can remember.

In another circle write some of the Ten Commandments, or, with younger children, draw the stone tablets and talk about what the commandments are. Explain that at the time of this particular Shavuot or Pentecost festival—the one after Jesus had died, come back to life and gone to be with God—his friends were together in a house in Jerusalem. Suddenly there was a noise like a strong wind from heaven that filled the whole house.

Fill a circle with swirls of colour for the wind. Explain that, as well as the wind, there were also what looked like flames, that separated out and came to rest on each person present.

Fill a circle with flames. Everyone was filled with the Holy Spirit and began to speak in different languages. People from all over the world were amazed to hear their own languages being spoken.

Fill a circle with as many foreign words as the children know. Explain that Peter, filled with the Holy Spirit, told the crowds who Jesus was, and about 3000 people started to believe in Jesus that very day.

Talk about the story

Use the pictures to help the children to make connections with other stories in the Bible as follows.

- **Harvest**: Why might God have chosen harvest time to send his Holy Spirit? Talk about the fruit of the Spirit (Galatians 5:22–23) and write the fruits around the harvest circle.
- **Law**: Why might God have chosen the time of remembering God's law to send his Holy Spirit? Talk about the way God puts his law into our hearts (Jeremiah 31:33) and helps us to keep it as his Holy Spirit changes us to make us more like Jesus. Draw hearts around the law circle.
- **Wind**: Where else do we hear about wind in the Bible? Talk about the breath of God or God's Spirit moving over the waters of creation. Explain that, at Pentecost, God made Jesus' followers into his new creation. Draw the world and other symbols of creation around the wind circle.
- **Fire**: Where else do we read about fire in the Bible? Talk about the fiery pillar in which God guided his people across the desert. Explain that God's guiding light helps Jesus' followers to know God's way. Draw signposts round the fiery circle.
- **Languages**: When in the Bible did languages tear people apart? Talk about the tower of Babel and how the Holy Spirit brings different people and nations together again. Draw lines from each of the border characters leading to the circle.

Ask the children to pick out what they like best about the Holy Spirit from the pictures they have drawn of him.

Play with the story

The outward signs of the Holy Spirit's coming were a strong wind, the appearance of flames, and the ability to praise God in new languages. In groups, create the sights and sounds of the first Pentecost and then be ready to use them as the story is told.

- **Group 1**: create a breeze with pieces of stiff card of varying sizes.
- **Group 2**: create flame effects by waving yellow, red and orange ribbons.
- **Group 3**: write words of praise on placards in four languages and then read them out in an ever louder chorus of international praise. Suggested phrases might be:

  - *Demos gloria al señor* (Spanish)
  - *Isus e minunat* (Romanian)
  - *Bwana Asifiwe* (Kiswahili)
  - *Stuti Hoos Prabhu* (Hindi)

Put the whole drama together to catch a flavour of what the people on the streets heard and saw.

Reflect on the story

Use some simple prayer ideas based on the following symbols of the Holy Spirit. If desired, use just one or two instead of all four.

- **Oil**: Fill a small bowl with perfumed oil, such as aromatherapy massage oil. (Choose one unlikely to cause allergic reactions.) Invite everyone to sit or stand and close their eyes, waiting for the scent to reach them. The oil is invisible but we sense its presence with us. Thank God that he is always with us through his invisible Spirit, even though we can't see him with our eyes. As a sign of inviting God's Holy Spirit into their lives, invite the children to smooth a little of the oil on to their wrist if they wish to do so. (Never apply undiluted essential oils to the skin. It is also wise to avoid the use of citrus oils on skin that will be exposed to direct sunlight.)
- **Water**: Set up a tray of sand, dry compost or stones to represent a barren desert, and a bowl of water surrounded by lush green pot plants. Provide plenty of small waterproof bowls or pots. The Holy Spirit

brings life to dead places, just as water brings life to a barren desert. Invite the children to think about places, situations or relationships in their lives that feel dry and dead like the desert. Ask God to make his Spirit flood into that place like a spring of fresh water. Invite the children, if they wish, to fill a small bowl with water and place it in the desert as a sign of their prayer.

- **Fire**: Cut some flame shapes from red or orange card or tissue paper. Display photos of familiar local places, such as schools, shops, your church building, the playground, the gym and so on, and others of different countries. The Holy Spirit brings fire, energy and passion to places and people who were previously humdrum and dull or loveless and afraid. Invite the children to pray for people and places by placing a flame shape on the place or places they would like God's Spirit to set alight with his love and courage.

- **Wind**: Provide a bowl of bubble mixture and several bubble wands, ideally situated near a warm air source such as a heating vent to give the bubbles more buoyancy. God's Spirit can lift a situation or relationship and take it to a new level, filled with life and hope. Invite the children to hold such a situation before God and breathe out their concern for the people involved by blowing into a bubble-wand and watching the bubble take on a life of its own.

— Theme 6 —

Hide and seek

Season: Summer term

General introduction to the theme

God sometimes feels very close, while at other times he seems to be out of reach. Sometimes he startles us by the immediacy of his presence but then he is gone again, drawing us on by his very absence. This has been the experience of God's people throughout history, ever since we first cut ourselves off from intimacy with God (Genesis 3), and it is just as true for heroes of the Bible as it is for Christians today. God wants us to 'live by faith, not by what we see' (2 Corinthians 5:7) because 'faith makes us sure of what we hope for and gives us proof of what we cannot see' (Hebrews 11:1).

Reflective overview

You will need:

A Bible, a large circle of black felt, 20 small pieces of black felt (on the reverse side of six of these should be pasted the following images: a star, praying hands, a dream bubble, water and a dove, a stormy sea, a mysterious picture of Jesus—possibly an icon)

Bible story: Genesis 15

Action: *Open up the Bible and then lay it down at your side.*

Script: God has given us the stories in his book to show us what he is like and how much he loves us.

Action: *Lay down the large circle of black felt and the 20 felt pieces around the edge.*

Script: Do you still play hide and seek? It must be one of the very first games most of us learn to play. Now you see me… now you don't. Peek-a-boo! It's a game with a purpose. Through it we learn to trust. Although something may no longer be in front of our eyes, it is still there, just out of sight.

Action: *As you talk, place the felt pieces on to the large circle.*

Script: It can be like this with God. Perhaps the game is a God-given lesson about faith that can help us through life. God is in all places and in all times. God holds everything together.

Action: *Finally, all the 'hide and seek' felt pieces are laid down on the large circle.*

Script: There's no place or experience where God is not present. Sometimes we are deeply aware of his presence and a moment of glory helps us know it. This inspires us and draws us on to seek God and live by faith from then on.

Action: *Search for the star picture piece, turning over one or two other pieces in vain first.*

Script: There was a person who was deeply aware of God's presence. His name was Abraham. Abraham lived by faith and obeyed God when he was told to go and find the promised land. He had a vision from God that changed his life. It led him on to seek God's eternal city.

Bible story: Genesis 32—33

Action: *Search for the praying hands picture piece, turning over one or two other pieces in vain first.*

Script: There was a person who was deeply aware of God's presence. His name was Jacob. Jacob lived by faith and dared to return to his homeland to meet his brother Esau. A strange thing happened by a brook that changed Jacob's life. It led him on to seek God and find it in the face of his own brother.

Bible story: 1 Kings 3:1–15

Action: *Search for the dream picture piece, turning over one or two other pieces in vain first.*

Script: There was a person who was deeply aware of God's presence. His name was Solomon. Solomon heard God speaking to him in a dream. It changed his life and led him on to seek God through his wisdom and writings.

Bible story: Matthew 3:13–17

Action: *Search for the water and dove picture piece, turning over one or two other pieces in vain first.*

Script: There was a person who was deeply aware of God's presence. His name was Jesus. When Jesus was baptised in the River Jordan, it led him on to seek God's kingdom at all times and in all places.

Bible story: Mark 4:35–41

Action: *Four pieces have been 'found' so far. Search for the storm at sea picture piece, turning over one or two other pieces in vain first.*

Script: There were others who were deeply aware of God's presence. They were Jesus' closest friends and, with him, they made new discoveries. Once they were caught in a storm on the lake and then everything was changed. It led them on to seek God in the life of Jesus.

Bible story: Revelation 1:9–20

Action: *Search for the mysterious picture of Jesus piece, turning over one or two other pieces in vain first.*

Script: There was a person who was deeply aware of God's presence. His name was John. At the end of his life, John caught a glimpse of Jesus. It changed him and helped to prepare him—and us—to seek our true home in heaven.

Action: *All the story pieces have now been 'found'.*

Script: I wonder if there are times when we have been deeply aware of God's presence. These moments of glory lead us to seek after God, making possible days and years of faith. God is still teaching us through his heavenly 'hide and seek' to trust him in the dark, to walk by faith and not by sight. God still comes close to us through the beauties of the world, the stories of his people, the life of Jesus, and the words and love of the people we meet. God is closer than our very breathing but also always just around the corner, drawing each of us ever onward to where we belong.

   I wonder if you have sometimes felt God to be very close…

   I wonder if you have sometimes felt God to be far away…

   I wonder what God is teaching you through his heavenly game of 'hide and seek'…

   I wonder where you are in his story…

The promise
The story of Abram at prayer

Bible link
Genesis 15

You will need:

A bank note, a bar of chocolate, some everyday objects (such as a wristwatch, flower, precious stone, cup of water), coloured pens, paints and collage materials, small gold stars and black felt, luminous stars, a large piece of card

— The Barnabas Children's Bible —

Story 13

Background to the story

Abram's experience of God in this story is one of several similar episodes in his lifetime. These were moments of glory when he heard God's voice for himself. Each time, Abram was promised a future, a home and a family, and each new vision helped him go on living by faith. God's promises were given again and again to reassure Abram and to keep him believing.

Even when baby Isaac finally arrived, Abram knew that there was still more to come. He still needed to go on seeking God and his true home in heaven. As the writer to the Hebrews puts it, 'Because Abraham had faith, he lived as a stranger in the promised land… Abraham did this, because he was waiting for the eternal city that God had planned and built' (Hebrews 11:9–10). In the story, God meets Abram and reminds him of God's presence and God's promise that one day he will have a great family.

Open the story

There are promises all around us in our everyday life, though we don't often realise it.

Show the children a bank note. Can they see the promise written on it? This bit of paper—and that is all it really is—is only valuable because of the bank's promise to back it up. Show the chocolate wrapper. Can the children see the small print that contains the manufacturer's guarantee? This is another form of promise. If there is something wrong with the chocolate, you can send it back to them and they will send you a new bar instead.

Many things are backed by a promise. God's love for Abram was backed by a promise and, like the bank note and chocolate wrapper, God gives signs of his promises. For Abram, these were the stars in the sky and a vision in the night. Later, God also gave him a change of name (Genesis 17:4–5) and a visit from three special people (18:1–15). God keeps underlining his promises.

Those who follow Jesus have God's written word, the inner witness of the Holy Spirit and the encouragement of Christian friends and family. God keeps his promises.

Tell the story

Today's story is about a time when Abram was worried about the future. God reminded Abram of his promise and helped him to keep going. Read the story from *The Barnabas Children's Bible* or Genesis 15:1–6 and 12–16, and then invite a volunteer to retell the story as it might have sounded when Abram told his wife Sarai what had happened that night. God pointed Abram up to the stars as a sign of the promise, and then, while Abram was in a deep sleep, God whispered more words of reassurance into his mind about the future. God is always willing to reassure us if we ask him.

God can speak to us through very ordinary things. He spoke to Noah and his family through a rainbow, to Balaam through a donkey, to Jeremiah through an almond branch, to Amos through a basket of summer fruit, to St Augustine through a voice in the next-door garden, to St Patrick through a three-leaf clover and to Mother Julian through a hazelnut.

Show the everyday objects and talk together about how God might speak to us through these things. Encourage the children to hear God's promises all around them through everyday things in order to help them live each day by faith.

Talk about the story

Play a game of cross the circle. Stand in a circle and then make certain statements. If that statement is true for anyone, he or she should cross carefully from one side of the circle to the other. For example, cross the circle if…

… you've ever made a promise.
… you're good at keeping promises.
… you've ever made a promise but failed to keep it.
… you've ever been promised something.
… you've been promised something and it has definitely happened.
… you've been promised something and it hasn't happened.
… you've been promised something that took a long time to happen.

Explain that Abram was given promises from God but they were a long time in coming true. Abram needed to be reminded again and again of God's promises. Ask the children what promises they make. What has been promised to them by teachers, friends or parents? What promises have they made to other people? How does it feel when promises are broken? Why might people break promises? Why do we need to be reminded of the promises given to us? What can help us to remember what has been promised us? Something written down… a keepsake… a ribbon… a bracelet or ring…?

Explain that faith means believing in what we cannot yet see because the one who has promised it is thoroughly trustworthy. Do some promises seem easier to believe because we trust the person who makes them? Share some promises the children have heard or you have made yourself. What sign would go with each promise to help the children believe in the promise? (For example, saying, 'I promise to pick you up at 3.30… and here's my mobile phone number in case I'm late.)

Play with the story

God used the stars to remind Abram not to forget God's promises. Stick some luminous stars on a large piece of card and then turn the lights off. Let the stars shine very briefly. Give the children a limited time to count how many there are before you remove the stars from their view. How many were there?

Out in the desert at night, Abram would have seen many stars. This was going to be a big promise! The stars would always remind Abram that God's promise was going to come true, even when there was no sign yet of a child on the way. Create a large 'starry night' collage, with groups of stars arranged to make some new Bible constellations that remind us of God's promises. For example, you could make a constellation shaped like Noah's ark, the burning bush, a staff or shepherd's crook, a sheep, a flame, a sword, a cross, or a dove. When the collage is completed, what might the children see to encourage them to trust God's promises?

Reflect on the story

Scatter some small gold stars slowly across a large piece of black felt. As you do so, read the words of Genesis 15:5–6. For Abram, these were his stars of the promise. His family would one day be as many as the stars in the sky. The stars can also be signs of God's promises to us. Each one can be a promise from God. Slowly read out some of God's promises below and invite the children in turn to pick up one of the stars, hold on to it and make this a promise for themselves. God says:

• I will never leave you or abandon you.
• I will always be with you.
• I will comfort and strengthen you.
• I will rescue you.
• I will hear your prayer.
• I will keep you safe.
• I will give you a future and a hope.
• I will lay down my life to save you.
• I will take you home.
• I will be your God and you will be my people.

After a pause, ask the children to replace the stars on the felt, saying out loud or thinking quietly about the particular promise that was special for them, which will help them to live by faith in the week ahead.

The fight
The story of Jacob at Peniel

Bible links

Genesis 32—33

You will need:

A dictionary, a rope for a sit-down tug-of-war, materials to decorate a prayer, cards with cartoon fight sounds on one side (see page 101) and a cross on the other

— The Barnabas Children's Bible —

Story 27

Background to the story

Jacob's life is an amazing story of mistakes, cheating, running away, disappointment in love, bad choices and exploitation at work, family argument and fear. It's a story of spiritual high points and great prayer moments, but also of faith forgotten, set against the backdrop of God's steadfast love. The climax to the story is an extraordinary wrestling match. Jacob wrestles with God in human form, or, rather, God wrestles with Jacob. A famous Christian writer, F.B. Meyer, sums it up by saying, 'This is life; a long wrestle against the love of God which longs to make us all his' (*The Secret of Guidance*, Cosimo, 2007). God never gives up on Jacob, however much he twists, turns and runs away.

Today's story is about God's encounter with Jacob at the River Jabbok, where God completes the long process of changing Jacob from a cheat into someone who is truly aware of God's presence and the part he has to play as one of God's people.

Open the story

Jacob's story is one of chase and catch up. Ask the children to sit in a circle with one child on the outside. The child on the outside moves round the circle and then taps someone on the shoulder. That person gets up quickly and tries to outrun the first child back to the vacated space. The child who reaches the vacant space first sits down and the remaining child is left outside the circle to repeat the process.

In the Bible, God is often called the God of Abraham, Isaac and Jacob. Sometimes, as in Psalm 46:11, he is simply referred to as 'the God of Jacob'. How amazing that God should be aligned with someone who was a cheat and a liar, forgetful and faithless! It shows us that God does not give up on such a person, preferring to spend a lifetime wrestling with him to shake him out of all wrongdoing so that he might cling to God alone. It is a very encouraging and hopeful title. God is prepared to wait a lifetime to bring us back to who we were created to be.

Choose a panel of three children who must each give a definition of an unusual word. (Use a dictionary for inspiration.) Only one child should give the true definition. Can the others work out who is lying and who is telling the truth? Jacob cheated and lied a great deal in his life. Today's story is about his encounter with God. The wrestling match is the moment when Jacob at last has to face the moment of truth.

Alternatively, divide the group in half and line up the two teams opposite each other. Starting at one end, a child calls out a word. The child opposite then calls out a word which is completely unconnected with the first word. Continue down the line in this manner. Anybody on the team can challenge a word that has been chosen at any point and try to prove that the word *is* connected in some way. Successful challenges score points for the team. Use the game to illustrate Jacob's way through life. It was full of unconnected twists and turns as he tried to dodge God.

Tell the story

Read the story from *The Barnabas Children's Bible*. In pairs and without touching each other, ask the children to create a slow-motion wrestling match. Explain that the place where Jacob's struggle with God took place was called Peniel, which means 'the face of God', because it was here that Jacob came face to face with God.

To demonstrate the struggle that is going on in the story, divide the group into two halves and hold a sit-down tug-of-war. (This is safer than a stand-up tug-of-war, but harder because there's no way to anchor your feet easily against the opposing pull.)

Explain that God wrestled with Jacob in order to help him to change. In the same way, even the best that we can do in life may be wasted if we don't allow God to wrestle us into being the best we can be. Sum up the story by chanting together the rhyming words below.

Jacob—wake-up
Jacob—shake-up
Jacob—take-up

For us, as for Jacob, the story is a wake-up to God's presence, a shake-up of our selfish natures and a challenge to take up God's way in everyday life.

In the story, it was God's way that worked, not Jacob's scheming. Esau didn't arrive with an army to attack his brother but with a welcome to forgive him. Esau's forgiveness was Jacob's new start. Now he really began to live by faith. Jacob even said that he saw God's face in the face of his brother (Genesis 33:10).

Again, play the word game above, but this time each word must be connected to the one before in some way. Point out that this is a picture of reconciliation rather than hostility.

Talk about the story

Jacob was on his way home when the wrestling match took place at Peniel. When Jacob had run away 20 years before, he had gone via a place which came to be known as Bethel. Bethel was the place of God—the house of God—the place where Jacob dreamt about an angel stairway to heaven. What a spiritual high that had been for Jacob, and what an important first step on his journey of faith! But perhaps that was all it had been—a first step on which he had remained stuck. Through all the years with Laban and despite all the wheeling and dealing in equal measure by both Jacob and Laban (the wives, the wool and the wealth), there is no real evidence that Jacob had grown in faith.

Talk about what happened to Jacob at Bethel (Genesis 28:10–22). Jacob was very deeply aware that God was with him at that time. He even made an agreement to give God back one-tenth of everything that he had been given. However, in the years he spent with Laban, it seems that Jacob had forgotten the moment when he saw God so clearly. He seems to have forgotten the impact of that moment—or perhaps he

deliberately shut his eyes to the moment when God broke through in his life.

Hot-seat the role of Jacob and question the volunteer as to why Jacob may never have told Laban, Leah or Rachel what happened at Bethel. Was he embarrassed? Had he forgotten? Did he think it was all a dream? Was it too mystical and mysterious to make sense any more? Why didn't Jacob pray? Why didn't he seek God after God had so clearly sought him?

Play with the story

The name 'Jacob' means cheat—one who grabs for himself and puts himself in pole position. Jacob's life was marked by cheating, deceiving and scheming. Jacob's encounter with God at Peniel was a life-changing experience but, before that event, Jacob prayed a long and beautiful prayer, which came about only because he was facing a crisis.

Read Genesis 32:9–12. Ask the children which part of the prayer they like best. Print out the prayer so that they can copy and illustrate a version of their own, perhaps picking up on just one verse. They could include a picture of the stone pillow where the promise was made (see Genesis 28:10–15), a walking stick, people and animals, weapons of attack or the stars in the sky.

Reflect on the story

Even after the prayer in Genesis 32:9–12, Jacob still didn't seem quite ready to trust God completely. He schemed and planned so that, whatever happened, the encounter with his brother might at least leave him with something of his own. He divided his property, sent gifts, split the family and manoeuvred for some sort of safe outcome. Only then, when he was left alone, did the wrestling God meet him. God wanted to change Jacob for the better. The midnight wrestling match was God's determined battle to rescue Jacob so that he could be blessed and changed.

Have a set of cards on which are written words such as 'Grrr', 'Pow', 'Wack', 'Thwack', 'Ugh', 'Ouch', 'Zap', 'Crunch', 'Wop' and 'Kerplunk'. Put a cross on the back of each card. Encourage the children to name some of the prayer challenges that are on their minds, such as prayers for peace where there is war, or for healing where there is much suffering. As they mention each issue, ask them to put down one of the cards with the wrestling sounds, as a reminder that prayer is a battle against all that is bad and evil in our world. After the prayers are finished, turn the words over so that the crosses are visible, as a picture that through the cross Jesus defeated all that was evil on our behalf.

Paul reminds us, 'We are fighting against forces and authorities and against rulers of darkness and powers in the spiritual world' (Ephesians 6:12). When we let God wrestle with us, he leads us to a new start and a new power, as he did for Jacob. Jacob never forgot the experience of wrestling with God. From that night he limped, and he had a new name—Israel—which means 'wrestled with God'.

The dream
The story of God's gift to Solomon

Bible links

1 Kings 3:1–15; 2 Chronicles 1:1–13

You will need:

Paper, pencils and pens, items for some simple challenges (see below), materials to make decorative bookmarks

— The Barnabas Children's Bible —

Story 147 and Stories 148–151 give examples of Solomon making wise judgments and also bring together some of his wise sayings from the book of Proverbs.

Background to the story

After seeing off various challenges from rivals for his father's throne, Solomon finally became king. What an inheritance he had! David had been much respected and had had a deep experience of God, so how could Solomon hope to follow in his footsteps? Solomon truly believed in God and wanted to be a faithful king (1 Kings 2:1–4; 3:3) but he must have been nervous. God had constantly spoken to David through poetry, shown himself through miracles of protection and blessed David with a deeply personal experience of God's mercy. Could Solomon be that close to God?

As Solomon began his reign, he must have longed for his own personal experience of the invisible God. Perhaps this is the reason for the extravagant sacrifices at the shrines, particularly in Gibeon (1 Kings 3:4). Are they evidence of Solomon's urgent search for God and his longing that God should not hide himself from him? It was at this point that Solomon had his dream. This is a moment when he felt particularly close to God and was offered whatever gift he wanted.

Open the story

Ask the children whether they can remember any of their dreams. Do they ever have the same dream twice? Are their dreams exciting or scary sometimes?

God often speaks through dreams in the Bible and that is one reason why it is a good idea to pray before we go to sleep at night. An ancient prayer of the Church (from the service of Compline) says:

From evil dreams defend our sight,
From fears and perils of this night,
Tread underfoot our deadly foe,
That we no evil thought may know.

Versions of this prayer, in both traditional and modern settings, can be found in Common Worship (Church House Publishing, 2000).

In Psalm 4:8, David prays, 'I can lie down and sleep soundly because you, Lord, will keep me safe.'

Tell the story

In Solomon's dream, God gave him a tremendous offer. He could choose any gift he wanted! I wonder what *we* would choose. Make a list of all the 'blank cheque' gifts the children can possibly think of—for example, tremendous wealth, superhuman power, to live for ever, perfect health, political influence, worldwide fame, artistic talent, enormous strength, unfading good looks. Ask the children to think of some of the powers that superheroes possess, to extend the list even further. Which gift would each person choose, and why? Which gifts would do the world the greatest good? Are there possible dangers lurking within some of the gifts?

Now focus on the gift that Solomon chose: the ability to know the right thing to do and to know the difference between right and wrong (1 Kings 3:9). Why might God have said that this was the best gift of all (vv. 10–11)? Now Solomon had had his own personal experience of God that changed him completely. It influenced the rest of his life and, even though he did not often experience such closeness with God again, he knew that God was always there.

Talk about the story

Collect a series of fun and challenging activities for the children to experience. Each one should have nothing to do with how knowledgeable a person is academically but much to do with other skills, and even common sense. Use the activities to talk about the fact that being clever is much more than just knowing things. Ideas might include:

- Bend your arm back and place a small sugar packet (such as those available from a café) on your elbow. Now swiftly move your forearm down and try to catch the packet in the same hand. Add more packets, one at a time, until you can't catch any more.
- In pairs, act out specific phrases for your partner to guess, such as zero gravity, walking the plank, making a cake, playing a sport, lighting a match and so on.
- Sign your name with both hands simultaneously.
- Keep three tissues afloat in the air. Start by throwing them into the air and then use one hand to pull them up each time they fall. You must not let any touch the ground. How long can you keep them all in the air?
- Raise your right hand and point in the air, tracing three imaginary squares, while counting to twelve (each number corresponding to a corner). Now raise your left hand and trace four triangles in the air, while counting to twelve. Now raise both hands. With your right hand trace squares and with the left hand triangles, and don't forget to count to 12!
- Bring both hands up in front of you. Now, with your left hand, point your index finger forward; with your right hand, raise your thumb in the air. Switch thumb and forefinger positions between hands. Do this as quickly as you can.

The gift that Solomon chose was wisdom—a word that is not very familiar to people today. Wisdom and knowledge are not the same thing. Draw two columns on a sheet of paper, one headed 'Knowing about things' and the other 'Being wise about things'. How are the two phrases different? Write up the children's ideas as you talk about them. When faced with a problem, how is wisdom needed and when is knowledge helpful?

Solomon wrote a lot about the difference between wisdom and knowledge. His writings are recorded in Proverbs and Ecclesiastes. Read 1 Kings 4:29–34. Solomon had so much wisdom that he became world-famous, and so he had power, influence and wealth too in the end, just as God had promised. He once wrote, 'All wisdom comes from the Lord, and so do common sense and understanding' (Proverbs 2:6). He writes more about wisdom in Proverbs 3:13–18.

The story about the two women and the baby in 1 Kings 3:16–28 is perhaps the most famous example of Solomon using his gift of wisdom. Tell this story, pausing before the end to see whether the children can be wise enough to work out what to do. The story is a good way into discussing what wisdom is.

After Solomon's dream, there were two more occasions when he experienced God's closeness. The second one was when the finished temple was dedicated (1 Kings 8:10–13), after which Solomon prayed an inspiring prayer. Solomon was indeed a very great and wise king, but being wise doesn't mean that we always act wisely and, sadly, this was true for Solomon. The third time God came close to Solomon was to warn him that he shouldn't get mixed up with worshipping idols (1 Kings 9:2–9), but Solomon didn't listen. Alongside the worship of the true God, he set up statues to the gods of the countries from which some of his wives came (1 Kings 11:3–8), and this was his downfall. Ask the children why they think Solomon wasn't so wise in the end. Is it perhaps easier to be wise for other people than for oneself?

Play with the story

Stories 149–151 in *The Barnabas Children's Bible* contain selections from Proverbs about families, friends and life. Read them or make your own selection from Proverbs. Ask the children which stories they like best. Now ask them to choose one or two each and create their own illustrated versions of the words, to make a display or their own book about Solomon's wisdom. Ask the children to think of their own wise sayings and decide on ten top pieces of wise advice that they would want to pass on to others. Write or illustrate them on some decorated card.

Reflect on the story

When we pray for other situations and other people, it is usually wisdom that we ask for, not more knowledge. Gather in a circle and put the wise sayings that you have written out and illustrated in the middle. Encourage the children to each pick out one (not their own, if possible) and turn it into a prayer for other people. Use the words of the familiar chorus about the wise man from the parable Jesus told, to sum up each prayer: 'The wise man built his house upon the rock... and the house on the rock stood firm.'

The beginning
The story of Jesus' baptism

Bible links

Matthew 3:13–17

You will need:

A well-known work of art depicting Jesus' baptism (download from the internet), craft materials, a bowl of water, a shiny surface

— The Barnabas Children's Bible —

Story 255

Background to the story

It is important that we mark special occasions in our lives, such as birthdays, festivals, anniversaries, starting a new school or beginning a new job. These times are important milestones on our journey through life and at such points we can sometimes be more aware of God's presence and blessing. Alongside annual festivals, many special occasions are celebrated in church, especially baptism, marriage and the dedication of a child. Beginnings are important and remind us that God is a God of new beginnings (Isaiah 43:19).

Jesus was fully God and fully human. The beginning of his adult life's work as a travelling preacher was marked by the special occasion of his baptism. As a boy, Jesus had been named and welcomed into the Jewish way of life with all the usual ceremonies. Now, at the age of 30, he was baptised at the start of his ministry. The story of Jesus' baptism demonstrates God's presence and blessing at this special moment.

Open the story

Begin by exploring memories and feelings associated with special days such as birthdays, a house-warming or starting a new school. Has anyone been to a baptism? This is perhaps the best example of a special moment marked by a party, prayers and possibly a new awareness of God's presence.

Tell the story

Tell the story from *The Barnabas Children's Bible* or Matthew 3:13–17. How might Jesus' baptism have been perceived by those who were present? For example, John might have been surprised to see his cousin coming for baptism. Jesus wasn't like the others in the crowd—the tax collectors, soldiers and Pharisees. How might John have described the event to others later that day? What exactly did the crowd see? Did Jesus look any different from others coming to be baptised? Did the crowd hear the voice from heaven? Did they see the dove or just a bird that happened to be flying around at the time? Were they cynical, uninterested or intrigued? Were any of Jesus' family present—his brothers or his mother? What might they have made of it all?

Divide the group up and ask them to think through the scene from these different perspectives, working out what different people would say. Once they have had a chance to chat it through, hot-seat some of the characters involved.

Talk about the story

It is at special moments that we can sometimes be particularly aware of God's presence. This was true for Jesus and it must have been a constant inspiration for him over the subsequent three years of his ministry. Interestingly, in John 10:40 we read that Jesus escaped Jerusalem just before the final Passover week, to spend time near the place where he had been baptised. Perhaps he needed to remember what had happened at the beginning. He would have remembered how the dove-like Spirit had come upon him and how God's voice had spoken over him, assuring him of God's presence and blessing. It is easy to see how important this memory would have been to Jesus.

One way to work with this story is to use one of the great masterpiece paintings of the event, such as *The*

Baptism of Christ by Piero della Francesca. Begin by showing the picture to the children and talking about it without any preconceived ideas or information. Ask questions such as:

- Why has the artist decided to interpret the story in this particular way?
- What extra details has the artist put in?
- How has the artist divided up the different parts of the canvas?
- What unusual features has the artist included?
- Which parts of the picture do the children like best?
- Which parts of the picture do they find strange or uncomfortable?

Use the discussion as a way in to asking the children to make their own pictures of the scene. What will they include or leave out? How will they present the story to show others what they feel about it and what it means for them? Alternatively, invite the children to reproduce a freeze-frame of the event on which the original picture was based, by becoming the people and objects in the picture. This can open up all sorts of new insights as the children decide together what movements and dialogue to include.

Play with the story

How can we hold on to the moments when God feels close and assures us of his love? Could we use a souvenir or special present from the occasion... a personal diary entry... a certificate or a card with an inscription... a badge or significant symbol?

What other keepsakes might remind us of times when God felt close? Could it be a pocket-sized cross, a WWJD (What Would Jesus Do?) wristband, a special precious stone, a lapel badge, a credit card Bible verse, or something else? Use the children's ideas as inspiration to make something that will help them when God seems to be far away.

Reflect on the story

Water is a powerful symbol at baptism. The new beginning is marked as a clean start, a moment of freshness and renewal. Gather in a circle and place a bowl of water in the centre, together with a piece of plastic or similar shiny surface. Invite each child in turn to dip a finger into the water and then to draw an outline on the shiny surface that relates to something they want to pray about—a person, a place or a situation. They can either share their thoughts with the whole group or draw in silence. Explain that drawing with the water in this way is a way of asking God to bring a new start for the situation which is being offered in prayer, such as a clean bill of health for someone who is unwell, some new way forward where there is a difficult problem to be solved, or a fresh idea of what to do next when asking for guidance. At the end of each drawing, say a pray together, such as 'Lord, thank you that you make all things new' (based on Revelation 21:5).

The crisis

The story of the storm on the lake

Bible links

Mark 4:35–41

You will need:

Some alarm clocks, a cushion, Psalm 107:23–31 printed off in large lettering, collage materials, colouring pens, a long piece of plain wallpaper, a large circle of blue fabric (like a mini parachute)

— The Barnabas Children's Bible —

Story 270

Background to the story

Jesus had had a very tiring day, telling parables about the kingdom. The boat trip across the lake with his friends was his chance to rest. He was so much in demand that he could rarely find the time and space on land for a quiet bit of shut-eye. The storm on the lake was a time of crisis that revealed something new about Jesus to his disciples.

Open the story

Hide some alarm clocks around the meeting area and set them to go off about five minutes into the session, during a time of general news sharing. Alarms are usually an unwelcome intrusion into a pleasant dream or a deep sleep. Today's story is about a rude awakening for Jesus, who was enjoying a much-needed rest at the end of a busy day. Talk about how it feels to be woken up in the morning. Does it make anyone feel grumpy? Is anyone still very sleepy? Is anyone reluctant to get out of bed? Or are they raring to go and start the day? Perhaps it depends on how tired we are and how well we have slept that night.

Tell the story

The story begs to be acted out, but this need not be complicated to organise. In Mark's version, there were several boats, which is useful if you have a large group to involve in the drama. Sit the children in small groups and let them imagine they are rowing out across a lake. One person (with a cushion) should play the part of Jesus. Another person could be on the tiller, another standing by an imaginary mast on the lookout, and the rest on the oars. Once the scene has been set, pause to interview the cast to find out what they are thinking about. Which of Jesus' stories can they remember, and what are their thoughts about Jesus at this stage?

Ask the mast lookout to describe the sudden onset of bad weather (a leader could play this role if needed). Build up the scene slowly, bad news on bad news, and let the others react as it becomes harder to row and they are increasingly drenched by the mounting waves splashing over the sides. Again, pause the scene and interview the characters. Point out that the disciples were experienced fishermen, so the storm must have been really bad for them to begin to get frightened. Now act the next part of the story as melodramatically as possible, with plenty of panic, shouting, emergency bailing of water, fear, anger and so on. Jesus goes on sleeping throughout the scene.

Pause the scene again and ask why the disciples might have waited until now to wake Jesus. What do they want him to do? Is he to be just another pair of hands to help hold the boat together, or do the disciples expect a miracle? Ask the children to say what they're thinking in the character of the person they are playing. Finally, act out the dramatic moment when Jesus stands up and tells the storm to be quiet. Explore the amazed and frightened reactions of the crew.

Talk about the story

Jesus was always with the disciples but today's story tells of a time when they were made more aware of his supernatural presence and the mystery of his true nature. It was a moment of crisis that revealed more of God in Jesus to his friends. It can be like that with us, too. God is, for most of the time, present but invisible during the routine of our lives. It takes a moment of danger and a cry for help, perhaps, to see God more fully.

Talk together about why Jesus asked his friends where their faith had gone. Would the boat have sunk if the disciples hadn't woken Jesus? Did Jesus want them to trust him without his having to perform a miracle? What might the disciples have learnt from the experience?

Play with the story

Psalm 107:23–31 is an example of thanksgiving that reflects the events of the story of the storm on the lake almost exactly. Print out the passage, verse by verse, on large pieces of paper with plenty of space around the words. Ask the children in pairs to illustrate each verse. For example:

- Verse 23: plenty of fish, ropes and nets
- Verse 24: some sea life and exotic coral and shells
- Verse 25: lots of waves
- Verse 26: a boat that is tossed and looks the worse for wear
- Verse 27: frightened faces
- Verse 28: prayer bubbles calling for help
- Verse 29: a peaceful scene with a becalmed boat
- Verse 30: happy faces
- Verse 31: shouts of praise in speech bubbles

Put all the verses together to create a long frieze that illustrates the story.

Reflect on the story

Gather in a circle and let the children hold the edges of the blue fabric. Ask them to flap the fabric to represent the storm at sea. As they do so, invite them to call out (or think about) all the things they are worried about. Then, when the leader says, 'Peace, be quiet', they should hold the material flat and calm, to represent the peace that Jesus brings, and say together something such as, 'We trust in God who stills the storm.'

Finally, give some time for quiet reflection on the story. This incident is very special to many Christians and helps them remember that God is always with them and can transform situations of fear and danger by his presence. Ask the children to think about what they like best about the story and what the story has meant for them today.

The end
The story of John's final vision

Bible links

Revelation 1:9–20

You will need:

Photos of celebrities, paper and pencils, items to represent Jesus' 'I am' sayings (see the suggestions below), A–Z street guide (see below), key outlines, silver foil

— The Barnabas Children's Bible —

Story 363

Background to the story

It seems that John was the only one of the twelve original disciples to survive into old age. He had been the youngest and now he alone was left from those first days. Some say that he spent many years caring for Jesus' mother (based on what Jesus asked of him at the cross in John 19:26–27). Tradition also claims that when he was a very old man, and during the reign of one of the emperors in Rome who was violently opposed to Christianity, John was arrested and exiled to the Greek island of Patmos. He may even have had to work in the stone quarries there in a prison camp. John's earthly life was almost over, and his present situation was dire, when he was given a glimpse of heaven that began with a vision of Jesus. The story of that vision was a moment of seeing the invisible that encouraged him to go on believing and made him ready for heaven.

Open the story

Collect together some photographs or pictures of famous people from magazines and newspapers. Place them face down in a pool in front of the children. Invite a child to pick up one of the pictures, making sure that the others don't see who it is. The child then has to try to describe the person in the picture, using only a physical description. Can the others guess who it is? How easy is it? If they can't guess, the child can give another type of description, focusing on the sort of things that the famous person says or does. Which way of describing a person makes it easiest for others to identify him or her?

Point out that there are no photographs or pictures of Jesus from the Gospel stories and no one really knows what he looked like. Unlike today's authors, the Gospel writers never thought to give us a physical description. It was what Jesus said and did that mattered. This is a real challenge to our present-day culture, which is very obsessed with physical appearance. Most modern-day representations of Jesus have their roots in the early religious art of icons, which showed Jesus in a particular way—usually with a beard and long hair, a long and stern face, and large piercing eyes that follow you everywhere. There is no evidence for this in the Bible. In fact, some of the even earlier wall paintings of Jesus in the Roman catacombs show him as a young man without a beard. What do the children think about this? Would it have been helpful to have a picture or photograph of Jesus? What would be the advantages and disadvantages of knowing what Jesus really looked like?

Tell the story

One description that we do have of Jesus in heaven comes from John's vision in Revelation 1:9–20. Tell the story from *The Barnabas Children's Bible* or from a Bible and then ask the children to draw up an identikit picture of Jesus from John's description. Ask them to make notes of what they hear and try to piece it all together. The key parts of the description in verses 13–16 are:

- He had a human form (he was the 'Son of Man').
- He wore a long robe.
- He had a gold cloth around his chest.
- His hair was white like snow or wool.
- He had flaming eyes.
- His feet were like bronze.

- His voice sounded like a waterfall.
- He had stars in his right hand.
- A sword came out of his mouth.
- His face shone like the sun.

All this is beyond imagining and so it is no wonder John fainted at the sight (v. 17).

What sort of identikit picture might the children come up with? Can they make a quick sketch? Are they convinced that all the imagery is an exact physical description? Do some things say more about the sort of person Jesus is than about what he looks like?

Talk about the story

When Jesus eventually speaks, he gives John something more to go on, including the words, 'I am the first and the last' (v. 17). We hear this again at the end of John's book (Revelation 22:13), where Jesus says, 'I am the Alpha and the Omega': this is another way of saying 'first and last' as they are the first and last letters of the Greek alphabet, like our A and Z. Talk about whether John recognised this way that Jesus had of talking about himself, starting with the words 'I am…'. John uses it often in his own account of Jesus' life, in which Jesus describes himself by a series of 'I am' sayings.

Collect together the items listed below, to represent each of the 'I am' sayings from John's Gospel. Lay them down in a line so that everyone can see them, as a reminder of the key statements that Jesus made about himself.

- A picture of a door or a model door from a doll's house ('I am the door')
- A good shepherd model or image ('I am the good shepherd')
- A bread roll ('I am the bread of life')
- A bunch of grapes ('I am the true vine')
- A cross ('I am the resurrection and the life')
- A road map ('I am the way, the truth and the life')
- A lit candle ('I am the light for the world')

To represent Jesus' saying, 'I am the first and the last', add an A–Z street guide of the city nearest to where you live. Allow everyone time to reflect on the different images and then ask which one the children like best. Which do they think is the most important? Which image is particularly special for them at this time?

Play with the story

Provide a variety of craft materials and invite the children to create a collection of their own 'I am' symbols to keep in a special box. This is a way of holding on to glimpses of God and helps us to go on believing in him even though we cannot see him.

Jesus also told John, 'I died, but now I am alive for evermore, and I have the keys to death and the world of the dead' (Revelation 1:18). This must have been a great comfort to John because, more than anything else, it confirmed that Jesus was the person he had always believed in—the one who had come back from the dead and would be waiting for him when John himself died. For now, John's present circumstances could only get worse, but this was not the end. Death would not have the last word.

John's vision came at exactly the right time for him and, through him, has been passed on to us so that we can go on believing. Cut out a key template from strong card for each child, shaping the part of the key that goes into the lock as three crosses. Cover the whole key with silver foil and decorate it. Use the key as a reminder that Jesus' death opens the door of heaven for everyone who believes.

Reflect on the story

Gather in a circle and place some of the 'I am' symbols, suggested earlier, in the centre. Invite the children to think about people who are having a hard time because of their faith. If your church supports an organisation working in difficult situations or you have links with Amnesty International, which campaigns for those who are imprisoned unjustly, allude to this organisation. Mention countries and people and, for each one, encourage the children to choose a symbol that they can put in the middle that would be a particular comfort to those people—or example, a lit candle for those who are suffering, to find a way through; the image of a door for those who are having a hard time, to find a way out; a bread roll for countries where it is hard to be a Christian, to have enough strength to keep going, and so on.

Bibliography

Barnabas books

Make & Do Bible Crafts, Leena Lane and Gillian Chapman (Barnabas, 2009)

Core Skills for Children's Work (Barnabas, 2007)

More Core Skills for Children's Work (Barnabas, 2010)

Caring for Others Today, Sylvia Green (Barnabas, 2007)

A-cross the World, Martyn Payne and Betty Pedley (Barnabas, 2005)

Messy Church, Lucy Moore (Barnabas, 2006)

Messy Church 2, Lucy Moore (Barnabas, 2008)

Not Sunday, Not School, Eleanor Zuercher (Barnabas, 2006)

Through the Year with Jesus, Eleanor Zuercher (Barnabas, 2009)

Footsteps to the Feast, Martyn Payne (Barnabas, 2007)

The Barnabas Children's Bible (Barnabas, 2007)

The People's Bible, Martyn Payne (Barnabas, 2010)

Websites

www.barnabasinchurches.org.uk

www.barnabasforchildren.org.uk

About
brf:

BRF is a registered charity and also a limited company, and has been in existence since 1922. Through all that we do—producing resources, providing training, working face-to-face with adults and children, and via the web—we work to resource individuals and church communities in their Christian discipleship through the Bible, prayer and worship.

Our Barnabas children's team works with primary schools and churches to help children under 11, and the adults who work with them, to explore Christianity creatively and to bring the Bible alive.

To find out more about BRF and its core activities and ministries, visit:

www.brf.org.uk
www.brfonline.org.uk
www.barnabasinschools.org.uk
www.barnabasinchurches.org.uk
www.messychurch.org.uk
www.foundations21.org.uk

If you have any questions about BRF and our work, please email us at

enquiries@brf.org.uk